KNOCKED OFF

BALANCE

Unexpected Events That Change

Our Course of Life

Clayvon D Scott Sr.

Knocked Off-Balance

Divine Alliance Publishing

Ordering information: Quantity sales. Special discounts are available on quantity purchases by corporations, associations, and others. For details, Contact the "Special Sales Department" address below: Divine Alliance Publishing   PO Box 383 Antioch, TN 37011 www.Divinealliancepublishing.com

Library of Congress Cataloging-in-Publication Data

Book Cover design by: Divine Alliance Publishing

ISBN 978-0-9861610-1-8

Printed in the United States of America

1. Title 2. Author 3. Christian life

FOREWORD

Clayvon Scott and I met at an unexpected place called Shelby Park. We both were lovers of baseball. In the summer of 2005, our spirits crossed paths. The ball park was perfectly located in Nashville, Tennessee on the eastside of the Cumberland River by the landmark overhead railroad tracks. We did not speak to each other much at first, but we did notice and observe each other from a distance. There were a lot of other coaches in the ball park but this guy stood out from the rest. He had the demeanor of famous football coaches such as **Tom Laundry and Tony Dungy**. These two coaches were exceptional at coaching the Dallas Cowboys and Indianapolis Colts respectively.

Clayvon Scott was a baseball coach and he was just as famous, at least inside Shelby Park, just as they were coaching professional teams. He was known simply as Coach Clay. He was a teacher, leader, parent, guidance counselor, a motivator, and coach all rolled up into one special person. Coach Clay had a special way of communicating to both his players as well as their parents. When he spoke before and after games to everyone, it was as though **E. F. Hutton** was speaking. Everyone stopped what they were doing and paid attention because what he said made sense. Not only did he give instructions about baseball, but he also shared life lessons that benefited all his listeners.

His new book is captivating. Not only will it touch many people's lives, it will give you an opportunity to listen, feel, and get to know Clayvon. I knew it was something special about this man. In this book, he depicts many real-life events that have changed the course of many lives. Even from the perspective of baseball, because in this sport, you never know what to expect from pitch to pitch, out to out, or from inning to inning. Any given pitch could be a bunt or a home run. The next out could be a double or triple play. The next inning could be the last inning or lead to an extra inning game.

Clayvon told me how special his journey has become with the writing of this book. He has grown spiritually and found a lot of resolve through trusting the Lord. To me, he already possessed that walk and spiritual nature. He exhibits his passion for Jesus like he did on that baseball field. I know you're going to love his book. Using the baseball analogy, believers in the Lord Jesus Christ shall not strike out. We are **NOT DESTROYED** even though some situations look bleak. Do not give up! It may be the last inning of a situation in your life, but you will not strike out with Jesus. You cannot lose the game of life.

When life knocks us off balance we can find reassurance in the word of God. However, we will need to mature in Christ and operate in His power in order for us to be able to deal with balance effectively. My hope is that you will read this book from cover to cover. It will reveal truths that will inspire you to live all of the days of your life knowing that Jesus is with you. Jesus gives us the strength that we need to endure to the end. We have a guarantee that he will be with us always. Everybody doesn't have this treasure but you can get it by believing and trusting in Jesus Christ. Ask Coach Clay because what he says makes a lot of sense! This book has the potential to inspire, motivate, console, and help you find peace and resolve. It may help you or someone you know regain that balance and **change your course of life**.

Reverend Thomas A. Cartmell Jr.

Associate Pastor- The Temple Church-Nashville, TN

Acknowledgments

I'd like to acknowledge Tonya Thomas for getting me started with writing my own books. Thanks to Divine Alliance Publishing for believing that I have a story worth publishing. A special thanks to my family and friends for sharing information and stories to put into my book. To my girlfriend, Alice Marie, who has been with me throughout this writing journey. She has helped me grow spiritually and has also helped me understand a lot of the scriptures. We have incorporated daily devotions and prayer into our life which has truly enhanced our relationship. Above all, I thank God for the guidance, courage, and strength he has given me. Without him, this book would not have been written.

Prologue

Birth and Death are natural occurrences, both move our emotions to tears. They could be tears of joy or sadness. **Death** is the #1 obstacle that we all face at some point in our lives. Whether expected or unexpected, it's heartfelt and never easy to get past. Oftentimes, some people never overcome the heartfelt emotions from the death of a loved one. Many unexpected deaths *knock us off balance and may inadvertently change our course our life.* Although we are given support, comfort, and prayer from family and friends, we struggle to get through it. *"He will wipe away every tear from their eyes, and death shall be no more, neither shall there be mourning, nor crying, nor pain anymore, for the former things have passed away." (Revelation 21:4).*

Unequivocally, death has a way of bringing family and friends together, and sometimes, tearing them apart. Many times, the very person who passed away unexpectedly, was the glue that kept the family bonded. Can you relate? The passing of a loved one is a time to put aside differences, opinions, judgements, and past hang-ups. Whether you're spiritually grounded or not, you'll take a moment to pray for the family. You offer comfort to help them through their rough times. The abundance of love and support is what helps the family regain strength and compose their balance.

What goes through your mind when the doctor tells you or a loved one that they have **Cancer?** Initially, it knocks you off balance. The doctor tells you that the current stage is treatable, but it will require some chemotherapy and a lot of changes in your life. You will need courage, strength, and discipline. Although many forms of cancer can be successfully treated, and possibly go into remission, you, your family members, and friends begin to prepare for the worse. The diagnosis is enough to change your course of life.

Unexpected blows can come from many directions. One least expected blow can start a chain of events. Imagine getting into an argument at work with your boss, and your actions, and or reactions result in the *loss of your job.* Upset, you leave the building and drive home recklessly, as if in a *road rage.* Unfocused, you speed through an intersection, drive straight through a red light, and cause a fatal auto *accident.* The aftermath is devastating. The long-term effects are the *deaths of a teenage boy and his girlfriend.* Spinal cord damage leaves you paralyzed from the waist down. One unfortunate, and unexpected chain of events has knocked you, your loved ones, and other families off balance. In an instant, everyone who is connected experiences a changed course of life.

This book will remind us all that life is full of *unexpected chains of events* that challenge us physically and mentally. We will be reminded of the realization that everyone gets hit with blows, and the effects are as devastating to others as it is to you. Our actions, and walk of faith amidst all, determines our recovery. Some people are much stronger and able to endure more than others. Many of us need help and guidance. It doesn't hurt to have Jesus Christ or a higher power to help us along the way. The ultimate question is, how do you overcome the life-long effects of devastation? The answer is, prayer and faith. If prayer and a walk of faith haven't been a part of your lifestyle, then maybe now is the time.

Table of Contents

Introduction

At some point in our lives, we establish a lifestyle that we consider normal. That norm can be based on our culture, demographics, race/nationality, religion, social status, financial status, education, wants, and desires. Once we determine our lifestyle, we follow a course of life that is normal to us. Oftentimes, some of us want to improve and or expand that lifestyle. Others remain content. As we go through different stages in life, our lives become a balancing scale. We began to balance life, work, school, church, wants, desires, needs, and more. What happens when obstacles are in our way? How do they affect our balance?

"Off-*balance is defined as: not well proportioned. not standing, sitting, or resting in normal equilibrium.   Upset from or in a state of confusion. Being in a state of surprise from an unexpected event(Merriam-Webster).*"

What unexpected events have occurred in your life that have knocked you off-balance? Have you gotten back on track? Have those events changed your course of life? Are you allowing those events to determine or shape your lifestyle? How have the events affected people in your circle? Has it created unbalance in people outside of your circle? What have you done or what are you doing to balance that scale again? Will you ever have balance again?

Here are some of life's obstacles that may knock us off-balance:

Health issues **Death** Mental/Physical Abuse **Stress/Anxiety** Work   Loss of Job   **Depression** Diet   Infidelity **Relationships/Marriage/Divorce**   Controlled   Unplanned-Parenthood   Acceptance/Denial   Education   Gang Activity Crime   **Police Brutality**   Incarceration   **Loneliness** Church/Spirituality   **Sexual Abuse** Past Hang-ups   Anger **Fear**   Identification Sex/Sexuality **Terrorism** Threat of War Racism/Hatred   **Physical Appearance**   Mentally/Physically-Challenged   **Gun Violence** Materialism   News/TV   **PTSD** Social Media   Nepotism   **Debt/Finances**   Lies   **Sin** Disobedience(Kids)   **Drugs/Alcohol-Abuse**   Wants/Desires Obsession **Jealousy/Envy**   Auto accident   Relocation Gentrification **Peer Pressure** Road-Rage   Embarrassment Politics Sex Trafficking **Poverty** Career-Ending-Injury(Sports) **Abandonment**   Natural Disasters   Displacement   **Bullying** Fires

Take a few moments to think about these obstacles! Does some of them resonate in your life? When the unexpected occurred in your life, did they lead to other events that caused your balance to become more uneven? Oftentimes, one obstacle would start a domino effect. Did it happen to you?

What do you seek to help regain your balance?

Medical assistance Interventions Institutions Meditation
Prayer/Church Forms of Relaxation **Job Change**
Reduction in Tasks Confide/Friends **Change of Friends**
Exercise Diet Marriage/Divorce Drugs/Alcohol
Acceptance Sex **Counseling** Prioritizing
Time Management Gambling **Compartmentalizing**
Education Upgrades and Eliminations Vacation/Getaways
Entertainment **Criminal Justice** Generosity
Revenge/Retaliation **Self-help/Perseverance** Jesus Christ/God

There are many solutions to correcting and balancing our scale.
Some of these can be very costly (not just financially), time
consuming, and exhausting but are worth it. Unquestionably,
some of the same things that knock us off-balance can get us
back in balance. On the other hand, there are also some
solutions that we hope to improve our balance, but those things
could have an adverse effect. Such as:

Drugs/Alcohol Generosity Institutionalized **Divorce**
Relocation Eliminations **Sex** Gambling **Acceptance**
Revenge/Retaliation **Confiding with so-called friends**

Is your scale balanced? How are you overcoming the challenges
when they arise? What toll is it taking on your life? What

changes and or improvements are you making? Of course, everyone doesn't have the same challenges in life but; at some point, there are unexpected events that cause us to have an uneven scale. Oftentimes, we allow the effects of the obstacles to determine our course of life. Some of those effects are positive and or negative.

When observing someone's demeanor, character, behaviors, achievements, etc., do you sometimes wonder what has their course of life been like? Do you have family members and friends whose lives have always seemed unbalanced and you're trying to figure out what happened? Has there been events that have caused you to ask the father almighty, "Why is this happening to me?" Or, "What have I done to deserve this?" Do you feel as though no one else could possibly be having a worse time than you?

In this book, you will hear events that may be much worse than yours. Some maybe similar or less severe. In the first three chapters, I will give you a series of events that determined my mom's course of life. You will hear how her children were affected by those events. The remainder of the book will be spin off chapters from my mom's journey that most of us have experienced at some point in our lives. You will also hear stories and events that I, other family members, and my circle of friends have encountered in our lives that have knocked us off balance. Many have restored their balance and carrying on with life. Others have never recovered from or are still dealing with the events. Some members in the circle are hung up on past events and can't seem to move on.

How do you press forward when the unexpected has occurred? Are you doing it on your own or with assistance? Do you pray and ask for guidance? Are you letting go and hoping God or a higher power lead the way? *"Being confident of this, he who began a good work in you will carry it on to completion until the day of Christ Jesus."* (*Philippians 1:6*).

As I reflect on my mother's course of life, I'd like to use the analogy **"calm before the storm."** Her adult life started out in marital bliss. She envisioned a life full of happiness and strong family values, just as she had seen with her mom and dad. There were a lot of loving, sunny days, and relaxing times. Rainy days would come but her mom said, "there be days like this." Then there would be thunder, lightning, high winds, hail, and tornadoes circling. At one time, the wind would blow so hard that it would cause a lot of displacement and collapse. *(Matthew 7:24-28).* The foundational structure was very weak.

Not sure what would happen next, fear and anxiety would set in. Sometime later, **torrential downpours** would fall and last for years-so it seemed. Multiple leaks would form from the roof. There's not enough pots and buckets to catch all of water before cracks and other damage is done. The rain has finally slacked off, the sun comes out again (*5yr Relationship*). Oh no, it's beginning to drizzle again. Mold and mildew is starting to take form. Now, mom is left disinfecting and cleaning, soaking up water, and **patching up the holes-all by herself.** There are only temporary fixes before more holes would form(**Dysfunction**). The remainder of her life would only have a few rays of sunshine to enjoy.

Here's her journey!

CHAPTER 1

BLISSFUL EXPECTATIONS

Elreta Marie McKnight was born and raised in Andrews, SC-a small town 50 miles southwest of Myrtle Beach. She was the 7th of 12 children born to Mr. and Mrs. Hezekiah Sebastian McKnight. One twin sibling would die at child birth while another would pass away before age one. Her childhood was a little structured with school in the church, bible studying, tending to the garden and cleaning the house for the girls, and working in the cotton fields for the older boys. Her mother was a beautiful, nurturing woman who loved her family. Her father was a hardworking, providing, and disciplined man who tried to instill the same in his kids. He established a **solid foundation** for his family. Mrs. McKnight would become very ill and passed away in her mid- 50's from unknown *cancer* while our mother was still a teenager. Her father would remarry before his youngest child was 18. Mr. McKnight would pass away a few years later from **kidney disease**.

Mom had already left the home to live with one of the older sisters in Robeson county, NC. Mom would blossom into one of the most beautiful young ladies in the area. While there, she would be courted by several handsome men, but she liked two who were cousins. One of them was well liked by her siblings because he was smart, **grounded**, and hard-working. Another was arrogant, spoiled, and very flirtatious. Of course, mom would fall for the flirtatious one. He would do all he could to keep her attention and keep her smiling. Mom would let him know that she is looking for a relationship that would lead to marriage. She'd let him know that she's not interested in being one of his girlfriends. He would assure her that she is the only one he needs.

In the beginning, he'd make her feel very special. They would go for short walks in the neighborhood and stop at the local parlor for ice cream sodas. Young men and women would stare as to say, "Wow, I can't believe she's falling for him." Although a couple of mom's siblings showed dislike for her future husband, they were glad that she seemed happy. Mom is expecting a life full of love and excitement. So, she would marry Mr. Scott in 1945. They were headed towards marital bliss, so it seemed. The first child would be born only 9 months later. Before you knew it, eleven kids were born from that union.

One would imagine with that many kids, that the marriage was going well. Truth be told, there were a lot of problems. See, my mother's husband was a spoiled young man who looked for every reason not to work an everyday job. His mom and dad would often come to his rescue when he needed money. As the marriage grew, his mom and dad couldn't help him as much because there were too many kids to help. Undoubtedly, Mr. Scott had to work to feed, clothe, and provide housing for the family. This was nothing uncommon or to be ashamed of, right. Any man who forms a family should desire to take care of that family. Unless, he's too selfish and un**grounded**. *"Do your best to present yourself to God as one approved, a worker who has no need to be ashamed, rightly handling the word of truth." (2 Timothy 2:15).*

Before Mr. Scott met mom, he was only working jobs where he could flirt with women and it never stopped even during the marriage. He would become a womanizer. He'd work in the cotton fields but spent more time flirting with the women than actual working. Word would get back to our mother about his flirting and arguments would erupt but later subside. Mom felt they needed to attend **church** and get more **spirituality** in their lives. Mr. Scott was very hesitant about going to church because he was afraid he'd see some of the women that he'd been flirting with. So, he would tell mom that I'll take you and the kids, but I don't want to go. Of course, that is not what mom wanted. She recalled how her mom and dad would attend church, hold hands, and pray. It seemed to help strengthen their marriage. Her father was proud to have his wife.

Later in the marriage, Mr. Scott would land a job with the Seaboard Railroad System. This was a stable job with good pay and very good benefits. The job would carry him up and down the east coast railroad. Although he could have taken a local position with the railroad, he elected to travel. This gave him excuses to be away from home while mom took care of the kids. He would come home after a week or two with just enough money to pay rent and feed the kids-playing no role in raising them. Oftentimes when gone for 2 weeks or more, he would lie to my mom and say, "there were rail problems up north that required extra help." See, my mom didn't have a phone where he could call. Nevertheless, he would come home asking her a lot of questions such as: "Has anyone been over here?" "Have you been anywhere?" Remember, my mother was a beautiful woman with long, black hair down to her lower back. She attracted a lot of attention when she was outside of the house. Men would stare and try to flirt while women would roll their eyes. There was one dark, handsome man, a friend of some of my mom's brothers and sisters, who would ensure he made eye contact with mom. They would have some innocent conversations when mom would go to the store.

In the early spring of 1955, Mr. Scott was M.I.A for months and left mom and the kids without money and food. She had to move her 8 kids in with her oldest sister. There was nowhere else she could go with 8 children. Her sister's kids were older and now out of the house. The sister never did like mom's husband. She'd often tell mom that *"he was a sorry piece of shit."* She'd say, *"if he ever came back over to my house that I'd kick his ass good."* Mom would sit in the house looking sad wondering what her life would be like if she married the smart, hardworking cousin but he was married now too. Her sister would invite the dark, handsome man over to talk to mom. She knew how crazy he was about mom. Sister would tell mom that he would take care of you and all the kids.

Feeling lonely, abandoned, and unappreciated, mom decided to go out with the gentleman. He was a single man with no kids. He owned a small store and had a small farm in the community. Oftentimes, he would give her extra food, offer to lend her money, and take her out for a drive in his car. Regardless of what's going on in her life, mom has some anxiety and apprehension on getting too involved because she is still married and skeptical of breaking her marriage vows. *"Give all your worries and cares to God, for he cares about you." (1 Peter 5:7)*.

Three months have passed, and no one has seen or heard from Mr. Scott. So, mom begins a relationship with her friend. A month later, mom is pregnant. ***What the hell was my mom thinking with her fertile ass!!!!*** She knew this was wrong, but she was unhappy and thought her marriage was over. Plus, she knew her husband had been unfaithful to her for years and has probably moved on. What she didn't expect was to get pregnant with child number nine. Condoms were not so readily available in these days and abortions weren't an option in our family. The boyfriend wasn't thrilled with the pregnancy, yet he knew mom was very fertile. Now, he has gotten cold feet about moving forward with their relationship. Mom would feel used and upset at herself that she became so vulnerable.

Six months later while pregnant, she'd get enough money from the now ex-boyfriend and brothers to rent a home in Richmond county, NC. **(Relocation).** A short time later, Mr. Scott's mom and dad would move to the same county. Suddenly, Mr. Scott would resurface after nearly a year. Fired from his job with the railroad and probably kicked out by his girlfriend. He begged and pleaded to come back. He'd tell her that he's done a lot of soul searching and is now a changed man. He'd apologize for abandoning her and the kids. He'd tell her that he's not upset about her pregnancy and he would take care of the baby as though it was his own. He'd tell her that his mom and dad sold their land in Robeson county and they are giving him some of the money to help with things until he can find work. Her sisters and brothers had warned her not to take him back if he comes home. ***Don't do it mom!*** As _Maya_

Angelou would say, *"When a person shows you who they are, believe them the first time."*

My mother, who was raised in the church as a little girl, was feeling some **Forgiveness**. She'd recall her marriage vows saying, "for better or worse." Plus, she'd blame herself for actions contributing to his abandonment. *"His leaving was not about you mom, it was about him."* (_Iyanla VanZant_). **Not your fault mom! Remember what your sister said about him!** Mom felt she had betrayed her husband also despite all his wrong doings. They both would apologize and ask each other for forgiveness. She'd think about it for the next few days. He'd bring things by for the kids. Mom would pray every night and ask God for forgiveness and direction as well. All she wanted was help raising the kids, to be loved and appreciated, have a stable home in a community where their kids could go to school regularly, and be involved in the church. Mom knew she'd still need some financial help and Mr. Scott was getting the support from his parents. Furthermore, he is the kids father and they are excited to see him. The next week, mom would let Mr. Scott come back.

A month later, in early February of 1956, the baby was born. Mr. Scott would carry on as the father and the kids didn't know any different. Mom is starting to feel that he is genuine about his iniquities and stepping up to the plate. *"It takes a strong man to care for someone else's child." (Quotes from*

Pintrest.com). Well, not exactly because he hasn't cared for
any of the other kids. So, this baby really won't be any
different, right. At least, mom is appreciating it.

They were making progress, so it seemed. A couple of the
kids were getting old enough to assist with chores and
babysitting. This allowed our mother a chance to work small
jobs like pressing clothes, sewing, and cooking for people in the
church. She was also getting a little time to fellowship with
some of the women of the church in hopes of getting some help
with the kids. You can imagine that she needed some help and
guidance for the kids because things have been difficult. Mr.
Scott would work a little in the local tobacco and cotton fields to
bring in money and stay closer to home.

Five years later and three more kids, it appears they were
on the mend. Mr. Scott was spending a little time with the kids-
mostly in a playful way. He was doing just enough to keep the
kids happy. But, mom was wanting him to be more of a
disciplinarian, take the boys under his wings, and teach them
how to be respectful, disciplined, and hard-working young men.
Avoiding confrontations, Mr. Scott would leave the house after
dinner and come home several hours later in a drunken state.
The drinking would become a regular thing. (**Alcohol Abuse**).
His behavior was changing, and he has begun to stay away from
home, days and weeks at a time.

Chapter 2

Abandonment (Torrential downpours)

One summer evening in 1960, the oldest son came home from working in the cotton fields and seemed very upset. When mom asked him what's wrong, he stated that the farm supervisor slapped him because he was clowning around with other workers. Knowing that Mr. Scott was in the field with him that day, she asked "Did you tell your dad?" He replied, "Yes, but he didn't say anything." When Mr. Scott came home that night, mom asked him "Why didn't you say something to the farm supervisor for slapping our son?" He replied, "He shouldn't have been playing around." Mom was irate and couldn't believe his answer. Some heavy arguing, even fighting would begin. Of course, mom was doing most of the hitting. When things calmed down for a moment, Mr. Scott would say, "Why don't I just leave!" Mom would state, "Huh, what's new, that's what you've always done?" He pulled out a suitcase from the closet and began to pack it with clothes. One of the older daughters came into the room and asked, "Where are you going daddy?" He responded, "I'm going out of town for a little while." Well, this time he didn't come back. That daughter would be 27 years old the next time seeing her father. He left my mom and the twelve kids in North Carolina for good this time and started a new life with one of his girlfriends in New Jersey. ***Wow! Can you say, "knocked off- balance!"***

Devastated, my mother struggled to figure out a course of action. She couldn't believe this was happening again. She was fooled to believe that her husband had sowed all his oats. Several months had passed and she hadn't heard from him. A lot of ***anger*** and ***anxiety*** had set in. Mother continued to pray and ask family for help. Now, she has exhausted all the financial assistance from family and friends. There are too many kids to move in with other family members. She is left begging for help. She managed to get some government assistance but only enough to feed the kids. Men, that knew her situation, would often come by offering help for other forms of payment but that was not the life my mother wanted to start. The oldest child is not even fifteen years old yet and couldn't work a regular job. Plus, that child is a pretty, young lady like our mom. Our mother did not want to expose her to the lurking predators around the community. So, our oldest sister and the third born sister would babysit other young siblings while mom ironed clothes and cooked for others to make money. The oldest two boys, fourteen and twelve at the time, would work in the cotton fields to help bring in money.

This pattern would continue for a few months, but the family was barely making enough money to pay rent and eat. There was never any extra money for clothing. So, you can imagine the *hand-me-downs*. Only four siblings were going to school, but they were not getting a good education due to multiple reasons (bullying, absenteeism, relocation, embarrassment, etc.). The older sisters are tired from the babysitting and not having time for school, reading, or anything else. The working brothers are becoming disrespectful and *disobedient*. They're spending some of the money to sneak around and drink alcohol and smoke cigarettes. They've started to miss work and are told not to come back. The fifth born son is getting sick every week and mom is forced to stay home with him. He is later diagnosed with *juvenile diabetes*. Suddenly, my mother is a couple months behind on rent, the landlord has told her to get out. With all the events occurring in torrential forms, our mother is stressed out-nearly to the point of a nervous breakdown and or *depression*. How is she managing to persevere? She continues to pray and ask God for guidance.

Heavy rain and storms are coming, and mom and the kids are not prepared for them. Mr. Scott didn't provide any groundwork or foundation. He has left them all unprotected. It's only a matter of time before the leaks in the ceiling become too much to stop. Cracks in the foundation have the home very unstable. The wind appears to be blowing the roof off. Satan is awaiting to devour all who are searching for an umbrella.

Trying to make ends meet, mom moved the family to another lower cost home. The home was in a community with more families and children for her kids to play with. The home was also near a church where mom and some of the kids could walk to. She would also ensure that the kids went to church and vacation bible study. Single men in the community would take notice of our mother as she walked to church and to the neighborhood stores, but afraid to approach her because of all the kids. Unfortunately, the married men would flirt more than the single ones.

In the early winter of 1962, mom would befriend a man who had given her kids money for candy and soda pops. Although he was a loud talking, attention getting man, he was handsome, and the kids thought he was nice. He and our mother would hang out a few times. Well, I believe you can guess what happened next. Mom is pregnant. She informs her friend and he tells her that he's married and doesn't want anything to do with the child. There were not many abortions done during these days, and mom didn't believe in it anyway. Feeling used again by her so-called friend, and disappointed in herself, mom wouldn't seek any kind of child support.

Mom is now becoming labeled by some of the women in the community as the *"woman at the well" (John 4:4-26)*, but in more of a sarcastic than biblical way. She only had a few friends and cousins in the neighborhood. A lot of women were jealous of her beauty and afraid to be her friend due to insecurities with their own boyfriends or husbands. Nevertheless, mom would continue with her life and do the best she could with her kids.

Summertime is approaching. Everyone is enjoying swimming in the nearby ponds, eating watermelons, and playing till dark. Our oldest sister is hanging out late with her boyfriend and is now pregnant at 16 but, she would move in with her boyfriend and get married after the child was born. The oldest son (15), not wanting to work in the cotton and tobacco fields anymore, has asked to go live with Mr. Scott in New Jersey. Initially, mom had some reservations about it, but the oldest son didn't want to go to school or work. So, she realized that living with his dad could be a good thing. The other kids didn't seem to be too upset about their oldest brother leaving. See, he was somewhat of a bully and acted as though he was the father when mom wasn't around. On the other-hand, he was a protector. He was not going to let anyone bother his siblings.

Well, in the spring of 1963, his protection or fatherly nature was needed. While walking home alone one evening, after hanging out with some of his friends, one of our brothers (age 11) was grabbed by a sexual predator. He was taken to a secluded area, threatened to be killed with a knife if he screamed for help, and **raped**. He would spend a few days in the hospital and the perpetrator would be caught and arrested. Although mom was distraught over this event, she was angrier at the man that vowed to love and protect her, and their kids was nowhere to be found. He could care less about what was going on in their lives.

Later that spring when school was out, the family would relocate back to the country again. They were living in a home with much needed repairs. The kids didn't seem phased because there was plenty of room outside to run around. A local man, who had his own home construction business, would hear of mom's situation and the needed home repairs. He had seen her before and knew that she was beautiful. He was a married man with two teenage boys. His wife was a distant cousin to Mr. Scott. Well, he would ride by the house and catch my mother at the mailbox and offer some to help with some home repairs if needed. He knew that she didn't have money to pay him. So, he'd tell her that some of her boys can help him pick vegetables and fruit from his garden as repayment. See, he also sold produce to some of the neighborhood grocery stores. Mom would often fall for the generous ones and it always seem to backfire.

Although this man had another motive too, he was different than the others. His handyman skills were a blessing for mom. She would always feed him when he came by and he loved her cooking. Although this type of behavior was common in these days, they were both out of order. He would bring her fresh vegetables and watermelons for the kids. He began to fall for my mom and a relationship formed. Although he was married, he led my mom to believe that his marriage was in the tank and would not last much longer. They'd carry on for five years. Three boys were created from their relationship. During those five years, three more siblings have left the house and moved to High Point.

After having the second of the three boys at age 38, mom's doctor told her that she probably won't have any more kids. She informed her boyfriend that she was done with kids and he would feel some relief. Well, with no hysterectomy done and no birth control used, she would get pregnant again and have her last child at age 40. Her boyfriend would become upset and say that mom lied to him. Although he acknowledged being the father, he used her so-called lie to get out of the relationship. He would tell mom that he and his wife are working things out. **Really!!! Were there ever plans to leave your wife?** Although mom was hurt, she never believed he would leave his wife anyway. She was more disappointed in his excuse and saying she was a liar. He would tell her that he'll bring money and food by every month for his boys but would not play a role in their upbringing. He'd ask if he could see the boys when he comes by and she would allow it.

In the winter of 1969, mom would move the remaining 11 kids to a new 5 bed room, 2 bath public housing in Hamlet, NC. Now, there's a little more comfort and stability. The oldest sibling in the house is the son with juvenile diabetes but now it's controlled with diet and insulin. He is going to school to work on his GED and working. All other siblings over 5yrs old are going to school. Mom and the kids are still not attending church but, mom has no transportation and she now feels as though she can't force church on the older kids. She much rather they get with friends and go on their own. Nevertheless, she continues to read her bible and pray every night.

We would stay in this house for six years. During that timeframe, there were a series of events and dysfunction. Two siblings would drop out of school at the age of sixteen. Mom was getting harassed by school truancy officials because two more of her sons were skipping school on regular basis. Skipping school was mostly due to ridicule and **embarrassmen**t. See, we were very poor and had to wear raggedy clothes and shoes-especially the boys. One son was probably the most gifted basketball player in the county but, quit playing because he

didn't have sufficient sneakers. The girl's clothing was over-
looked at times by the schoolboys because they were pretty
with cute shapes and mom would ensure their hair was nice.

In early 1970, the oldest daughter's husband was shot
and killed in High Point, NC (**Gun Violence**). She would become
too distraught to take care of her kids (ages 4 and 7). Mom,
being the caring and concerned person she's always been,
brought them into her house. **Whew, if the house wasn't
already full!** Mom didn't want two of her first grandbabies to go
to a foster home because she had heard a lot of bad stories
about them from her parents. Plus, the granddaughter was very
pretty, yet fearful and fragile. Oftentimes, she would cringe at
the tone of one of our older brother's voice when he came to
visit us. That brother had lived with our oldest sister and her
husband briefly and would babysit before her dad was killed.
Why was she so afraid of him?

In the late winter of 1970-71, two of the daughters
would get pregnant at the age of 15 and 16. Their boyfriends
were not ready to become fathers, so the babies would stay in
the house too. If these events weren't enough to swallow, the
father of mom's last three kids would come by in a drunken
state and try to get her to sleep with him. She was not going
there anymore. So, he would get upset. He'd inform her that he
was not giving her any more money because it was being used

to feed everyone in the house. He would tell her to put her free-loading ass kids out or force them to work.

Over the next few years, things would remain relatively calm, except for the harassment from truancy and the property housing officials. Mom's kids were still skipping school and now hanging with the wrong crowds. The housing authority was wanting to come into the house for random inspections. Some of the jealous people in the neighborhood were tipping them off on the amount of kids that were in the house. When mom was awarded the house, the housing authority informed her that 12 was the maximum allowed in the 5-bedroom house. Well, we were up to 16. They would threaten mom to reduce the headcount or find somewhere else to live. Worried and not knowing what to do, mom would mention this to some of the older siblings in the house and to family members to see if they had any solutions. One of our uncles agreed to let one of the daughters come live with his family because he and his wife worked at night and needed someone home with their kids. Another daughter would take her baby and move in with her boyfriend.

Mom would continue to be harassed by the housing authority and she tells them that she is almost there. Another daughter is getting close to moving into her on place with her two kids. Although this was not the life mom envisioned, this housing arrangement was the most conducive for her kids. The space and atmosphere were giving her room to sort things out.

Over the next six months, two teenage sons would go to juvenile boot camp due to missing school. The oldest sister who is unstable from the death of her husband and *physical abuse* from her last boyfriend is pregnant with her fourth child and needs a place to live. Her two oldest kids are gone from the house and now adopted by their dad's parents. The housing authority officials are harassing mom even more now because a couple of the kids are now adults and they are wanting to increase the rent by nearly 50%. Unfortunately, the harassment would become to over-bearing and mom would move out.

In the spring of 1975, one of the sisters moved into her own place with her two kids. A couple months later, she got a ride to the local Cafe to get her favorite sandwich and hang out with some friends. Prior to arriving, a young lady had just been told to leave the Café because she was too drunk, loud, and disturbing other customers. While the drunken lady was outside, she began cursing and throwing beer bottles and bricks at the building. One of the bricks would break a window and the owner called the police. The owner would describe the young lady to the dispatcher as the police were in route. Just as the police were arriving, our sister was coming outside with her sandwich! The police thought she was the culprit. So, one of the officers grabbed her-yelling and cursing her, he tried to subdue her. She escaped his grip, pushed him, and took off running. Pissed, the officer drew his gun, yelled for her to stop, then fired his weapon striking her in the back, left shoulder (*Police Brutality*). **Can you say knocked off balance!**

Mr. Scott left the house and everyone in it unprotected. Satan would climb through the windows and create a lot of havoc. Even when the sun was shining, there was dysfunction. Mom could not cover and guide each of her kids. One or another would be left unprotected, but she would pray and ask for guidance. *"Whoever dwells in the shelter of the highest will rest in the shadow of the Almighty. I will say of the Lord, He is my refuge and my fortress, my God, in whom I trust. Surely, he will save you from the fowler's snare and from the deadly pestilence. He will cover you with his feathers, and under his wings you will find refuge. You will not fear the terror of night, nor the arrow that flies by day, nor the pestilence that stalks in the darkness, nor the plague that destroys at midday." (Psalm 91:1-6).*

Chapter 3

Perseverance: Patching the Holes

Over the next few years, we would move around in Hamlet several more times. Mom would continue to do the best she could with raising her kids. El, the son with diabetes, would play a pivotal role during that timeframe. He was a very intelligent man who strived to learn different things. Plus, he was the only one with a driver's license. He would go to work in the mornings and get off around 4pm. He would take mom and other siblings where they needed to go. He had a fatherly nature and all the siblings under him gave him much respect. He'd tell us stories-serious and funny ones. He would lecture us on the importance of "doing for others as you would want them to do unto you." He'd say, "Grow up and be prosperous young men and women, never take life for granted, get an education because you will need it down the road!" He was right.

We always knew there was something very special about El. I didn't realize until I began to write this book, that El was one of the only child who went to church regularly as a young boy. He was not pressured by mom or anyone else. He looked forward to his grandfather coming to pick him up for church. Maybe his illness provoked him to seek more spiritual guidance. Despite his health and other challenges, he remained steadfast and never took life for granted. For that, we had more love and respect for him. *"Everything in the world is about to be wrapped up, so take nothing for granted. Stay wide-awake in prayer. Most of all, love each other as if your life depended on it. Love makes up for practically anything. Be quick to give a meal to the hungry, a bed to the homeless-cheerfully. Be generous with the things God gave you, passing them around so all get in on it."* (1 Peter 4:7-10).

By the late 70's, all the remaining children in the house, except for the youngest son, were working. Mom would not allow him to work because of allergies. He would stay home with her during the summer-helping with cleaning and washing clothes. She would have small talks with him about life. He would listen more than talk, but paying attention. He would run small errands for her while she prepared to cook dinner for everyone. Nevertheless, some of the kids had regular jobs while others worked in the tobacco and peach fields. They would give mom money for food and other needs. Mom would make a couple of the brothers give the youngest son a few dollars as well. They would have an attitude about it, but she'd inform them that he does things around the house for everyone while they're working. **"Spoiled is what he is"**, they'd say. Also, they would use some of their money to buy their own clothes which was a big help too.

By now, mom is in her early 50's. She could probably work somewhere herself but there is some fear and anxiety about starting work so late in her life. Plus, she now has a boyfriend who is working and helping support her. Furthermore, she is exhausted mentally and physically from the events in her life. From time to time, mom would use her skills of sewing, ironing, and cooking to make extra money in the neighborhood when everyone was at work or school. I'm not sure if mom envisioned being a housewife her entire life, but this is what was happening for many women during this era. Unfortunately, mom's situation was different than most. She would continue to pray for increase, guidance, and endurance every night.

As years passed, mom would continue to have some anxiety. She would break up with the boyfriend due to his jealousy and alcohol abuse. She has learned her lesson with the men that's come into her life, and she has made the decision to do without them. She would continue to finish raising her kids alone. Some of her children were doing well. Several would graduate from high school, enter the job world, start families, and get married. On the other hand, several were suffering from a multitude of issues. Depression, drugs, alcohol, and PTSD were taking a toll on several siblings. There would be a few trials and tribulations along their journey but none too devastating. A couple brothers would be *incarcerated* for minor crimes. Thank god, there were no drug charges, gang violence, or murders. Several siblings would migrate to New Jersey upon graduating high school and start families. Surprisingly, their dad would let them live with him and his girlfriend until they found a stable job and a home, but he had motives.

In 1984, our brother with diabetes would lose his eye sight. Although it was a major occurrence, he would remain in good spirits. Mom and other siblings would take care of him. At the beginning of his eyesight loss, mom would administer his insulin (by syringe). Later, he would insist on doing it himself. We'd all monitor him for a while to ensure there were not any problems, but he was handling it well. Even though he was blind, several of us would go to him for advice. You could tell that it made him feel good to help us especially the youngest three boys. He would even give mom advice too. El was wise beyond his years.

In 1986, the last of mom's sixteen children was graduating high school and receiving a basketball scholarship to further his education at Tennessee State University in Nashville, Tn. Mom was proud and sad at the same time. Her baby is leaving home, but she knows he is becoming a man. *"Show yourself in all respects to be a model of good works, and in your teaching show integrity and dignity." (Titus 2:7).* There would be other proud moments to follow as other siblings decided to go back and further their education as well. Although none of the siblings had any interest in joining the military, several were listening to our brother El when he spoke of furthering their education. By 1992, three other college degrees, several certifications, and job promotions would come. Mom would take her first long road trip, as she would travel 500 miles to be a part of her youngest son's wedding.

Upon returning home from her long road trip, one of her older sons would have his second stroke due to complications from **hypertension**. His recovery would take several months. His girlfriend in High Point is overwhelmed and can no longer take care of him. So, he moves back to Hamlet. Although he has his own place and can get around on his own, mom is bringing him food, washing his clothes, and ensuring he is taking his medicine. As he gained strength, he informs mom that he can do for himself. Though he is somewhat crippled and walking with a cane, he'd walk several blocks daily to her house just to keep her from coming to check on him. He'd let her know that she's done enough.

In 1995, all sixteen siblings and mom would gather

together for a reunion and family portrait. What a proud moment! **Mom, you've done a great job**. Good thing we got together that year because in 1997, we would lose our brother, El, to complications from Diabetes at age 47. Mom was distraught for a long time following his death. To add insult to injury, three other sons and a daughter, unhappy with their current situations, would get hooked on "**crack cocaine**." Mom would have constant anxiety for the next few years. Her anxiety has now triggered some health concerns. She is having constant heartburn, upset stomach, acid reflux, and rise in her blood pressure. She would not go to a doctor. She'd use old remedies and over-the-counter meds to reduce her symptoms.

In 2003, mom would have what appeared to be a stroke. She would go into a coma and be transported from our local hospital to Presbyterian Hospital in Charlotte, NC. After extensive tests, doctors discovered that mom's small intestines were severely damaged and become gangrenous. The gangrenous had poisoned her bloodstream and needed to be removed. Following surgery and numerous meds, mom would slowly gain consciousness but remain in the hospital for 3 weeks. There was a lot of prayer and comfort from family and friends. What a huge sigh of relief and honor to God! Mom would slowly recover at home and seem to be returning to her ole self.

Later that year, the father of her last three sons would pass away from *prostate cancer*. May of 2004, her oldest son would pass away from *cirrhosis* at the age of 56. Unable to attend the funerals due to her recovery, mom would stay at home with one of our other siblings. Four months later, on a mid-September night, I called mom to see how she was doing. She'd say, "I'm doing ok." We would talk for fifteen minutes or so. Suddenly, mom started slurring words and now no sound at all. I'd keep saying, "mom, mom, mom." No response! Then I would yell, "Mommmmmmm…….." Finally, I hung up the phone and called a sister who lives a couple blocks away and told her that something is wrong. She responded and said, "it's storming a little bit here and maybe it has affected the phone line." I replied, "No, she was slurring before she stopped talking." I asked her to call another brother to go by and check on her. He did and found mom slumped over on the couch with the phone in her hand. 911 was called and mom was rushed to the hospital. She would pass away the next day at the age of 77. **"Can you say, Knocked off-balance."** Although mom was the last of all her siblings to live, she was still gone too soon.

When I think about mom's last breath on earth, I reflect on the spiritual song by _James Cleveland_, _"I Don't Feel No Ways Tired."_ It epitomizes mom's perseverance and love for the Lord. Take a moment to look up the song! Here's the beginning of the chorus! _"I don't feel no ways tired. I've come too far from where I started from. Nobody told me that the road would be easy. I don't believe he brought me this far to leave me."_ This song would be sung at her funeral by one of her sons-in-law. Can you imagine the heartfelt moments following this song?

Most of mom's adult life was unbalanced. We can't judge her by the mistakes and or events that took place. The thing that we can judge, is how strong mom was. Being able to keep her sanity and **persevere** through all the events was unimaginable. She never asked for anyone to pity her life. She stood up like a "Big Girl" and did what she could. Although today many women are much more independent than in the 60's, 70's, and 80's, do you think many of them could withstand the events my mom endured. She was the most courageous, loving, caring, and nurturing woman you'd ever meet.

Mom, you exemplified the patterns of a _Proverbs 31 Woman_. It's unfortunate that Mr. Scott didn't realize what he had. Elreta Marie McKnight-Scott, you were a phenomenal woman. Those that didn't know your path would have never known that your life's journey was full of "**_unexpected events that knocked you off-balance._**" Although your course of life was determined by these events and you grew weary at times, you kept your faith. _"Do you not know? Have you not heard? The Lord is the everlasting God, the creator of the ends of the earth. He will not grow tired and weary, and his understanding no one can fathom. He gives strength to the weary and increases the power of the weak. Even youths grow tired and weary, and young men stumble and fall; but those who hope in the Lord will renew their strength. They will soar on wings like eagles; they will run and not grow weary, they will walk and not be faint." (Isiah 40:28-31)._

Chapter 4

Relationships-What's the Ultimate Goal?

When some of us reach a certain stage in our lives, we start to seek out someone that we'd like to share good times with (dates, conversations, etc.). Nowadays, it's a little easier meeting people with the internet, Facebook, and dating sites. Of course, there are some risks. Nevertheless, those meet and greets could lead to friendships, relationships, or nothing at all. Through conversations and hanging out, we learn more and more about that person. We learn each other's likes and dislikes, what type of background you're from, financial and social status, how grounded you are, what's your current relationship status, have you and your ex moved on, are there kids, sexual health, etc. After learning these things about each other, now we know you, so we think. Then one thing leads to another. Now, the assumption is that we're clicking. Suddenly, *intimacy and sex* take place. **Are we in a relationship?**

One of the things that we often fail to do in the conversations is communicate what our goals and expectations are before the very close and personal interactions. Now,

43

emotions and feelings arise and you're not ready for that. When Mr. Scott was courting mom, she wanted to be clear on the goals and expectations. She was not going to be sleeping around with no goal in site. Marriage was her ultimate goal and she made sure it was understood. We should all be clear with our communication when it comes to potential relationships. If you want to date and hangout, then say it. If you're interested in having a sexual relationship with no strings, say it. Oftentimes, that person may have the same ideas. Now, this may not be the **Bible's** way of doing things, but it gives transparency. So, use that courage and candor to communicate your objectives and don't lead the person on to thinking it's something more. Don't **knock** someone's life **off-balance** because you looked at them as a conquer while they were assuming a relationship!

Now, believe me, you can communicate the expectations and act differently which causes confusion too. Sometimes, we realize that we have a good person and we don't want to commit to anything, yet we don't want to lose them either. You know you can't give them what they'd like but you do just enough to keep them from someone else. *"Though he desires it and will not let it go, but holds it in his mouth."* (*Job 20:13*). Can you say selfish dog! Some may reference this as *"having your cake and eating it too."*

Since divorcing, I've been out here dating for five years now. I knew there were a lot of beautiful, single women out here, but you become somewhat oblivious when you're not looking for anyone. Nevertheless, the women were looking, and I was flirting. Coming out of a twenty-year marriage, I was not ready to begin anything serious. In fact, I'm not even ready to work towards a relationship. Initially, I was just looking for someone to hang out with and have some fun. I would communicate these things as well. Most women would appreciate my honesty, yet they'd feel bad for me because of my marriage ending. See, many of them had been hurt from relationships or marriages too, but their relationship was not twenty years long. They were tired of the same old lies from men who were just out to get what they wanted. Because of that honesty, some were cool with just hanging out. They'd enjoy a good movie and dinner, dancing, and a good laugh. Due to the treatment and feeling appreciated, things would lead to intimacy. Oh, oh!! Can we keep the emotions in check?

We all feel the need to be wanted and desired regardless of the circumstances. It may not be God's way but it sure does make you feel good. Even if it's only for a little while. For the most part, I was not much different than the other guys except for honesty. As I began to enjoy more of one woman versus the other, I'd begin to treat them very well. I was a good listener and very thoughtful. I'd remember what they'd like and or like to do and make it happen. Suddenly, I am carrying on like it's a relationship. Before things would get to deep, I would break it off and move on. This pattern would repeat with several different women yet keeping them as friends. I was not living right. I'm out here sleeping with multiple women and leading them on. Then hurting their feelings causing some temporary *balance* issues in their lives. I was wrong for this.

They didn't hate me afterwards because I was honest with them, but my actions showed differently. Several of the women that I dated were marriage material. Although they all would tell me that I'm a good man, a good catch, and shouldn't be available, one of them let me know that I'm going to miss my blessings with this type of pattern. I was carrying on as though I was a player-even though, that was not my nature. You see, I considered myself as being marriage material too. Not to sound conceded, but I'm made for one person at a time, not multiples.

Good thing I've been looked upon as a nice guy. Undoubtedly, these encounters and let downs could have went the other way. The women could have been extremely angry and retaliatory. I did have one stalking encounter for which the police were called but it ended up being a misunderstanding or poor communication. Whew! Occasional unprotected sex could have led to **STD's** or even worse. I can't say pregnancy because I've had a ***vasectomy,*** but this could happen to others. Have you had any bad encounters?

A daughter of one of my work colleagues had a relationship encounter that went the other way. She was a beautiful, athletic, young lady who had just finished high school and preparing for a basketball career in college. She's hanging out at her little cousin's baseball game one spring day and meets a handsome young coach who she calls "Prince Charming." She's amazed how good looking he is and that he's interested in her. Well, hanging out with him and having good conversations would lead to sexual encounters. A couple months later, she gets sick and initially the doctors can't diagnose the illness. A week later, the bloodwork comes back, and she is HIV positive. ***Can you say knocked off-balance!*** She knew that Prince Charming was the only person she had been with. Now, her life is changed forever.

I purchased her book to support her and her cause. Little did I realize that I knew her Prince Charming. He was one of the coaches at the same park where I coached. The little cousin that she was coming to watch was on my baseball team. Wow! Nevertheless, there were two other women at the park who Prince Charming had allegedly been seeing as well. I'm not sure if he was sleeping with them, but after the book came out, all three of them disappeared from the park. I hope their lives weren't knocked off balance too. I haven't seen Prince Charming in many years. I'm told he is now married with a child and I'm not sure if he has ever developed HIV symptoms but apparently, he's a carrier.

Although her life was torn apart, Miss Brown didn't let the illness take her into a state of depression. In fact, she is now an author and motivational speaker. She has appeared on several television talk shows including the Oprah Winfrey show, MTV, and BET telling her story. She travels around the country speaking to outreach groups on **HIV/Aids**, protection, abstinence, trust, and relationships. She gives thanks to her family, friends, and counselors for all the love and support. Above all, she praises God for helping her through her darkest times. *(Naked Truth by Marvelyn Brown, 2008).*

There could truly be some consequences when dating multiple people or sleeping around. I'm not sure if things occurred with Mr. Scott. It's been said that he had another child too. One of my older brothers grew up to become a womanizer like his dad. There were some consequences to his encounters. He was stabbed, had his throat cut, and nearly killed due to sleeping around with multiple women as ex-boyfriends exhibited envy and jealousy. He was a handsome, curly-headed, and muscular built young man. He was very charming and flirtatious-just like his father. He'd live with one woman and sleep around with several others. He struggled to hold a regular job but good at handyman work. So, you can imagine how some of his relationships were started. He'd often be at home during the day while the ex-boyfriends were at work. Hmmmm......Was he emulating his father!

After being separated and out of the house for six months, I ran across an old female friend from college. She was surprised to find out that I was divorced. We exchanged phone numbers. Through conversation, I'd inform her that I am not looking for anything and not ready for a relationship. She said that she understood, and she wasn't either following a messy relationship. But she said that she would love to see me again. Well, the next meeting would take place at my apartment and one thing would lead to another as you can imagine. We enjoyed each other's company. Before she left for the night, she jokingly said, "don't ignore me after tonight." I said, "I won't."

We'd talk and text a few times over the next week but I'm still looking and chatting with other women on dating sites. A couple weeks later, she invited me to her house on a Sunday evening. Following dinner and a couple glasses of wine, more **fornication** occurs. An hour or so later, my asthma flares up. See, she has a couple of dogs that are generally all over the house. I began to sneeze and wheeze. I needed my inhaler but it's at my place. I'd try to tough it out, but it was too much. I informed her that I must go and said we will talk tomorrow.

The next day, she would send me a good morning text and I responded with the same. Over the next few days, we would text but no true conversation. A week later, we've only had contact once. She became anxious. My work days were long plus she knew that I spent time with my kids during the week and every other weekend. As the week went by, I didn't respond to a couple of text and calls. She began to feel ignored.

About one o'clock the next morning, I get a buzz from the gate of my apartment. I thought, "someone must have the wrong number." So, I went back to sleep. Approximately thirty minutes later, there's a knock at my door. She's calling my name but not very loud. Upset that she came by unannounced, I ignored her and went back to bed. I didn't buzz her in, so she must have followed someone through the gate. *"And if anyone will not receive you or listen to your words, shake off the dust from your feet when you leave that house or town." (Matthew 10:14).* She left but I'm sure she wasn't feeling this scripture.

Later that day, while I was at work, she sent me a text and said she came by and wanted to see if I was ok. I played it off and said, *"I'm ok but when did you come by."* She asked if we could talk later and I said ok. That night, I had another date and didn't respond to her text that night. She came and buzzed the gate again around 11pm. I was in the complex but not at my apartment. An hour later, there was another buzz. Finally, she sent a text message cursing me. I leave my date's apartment around 1:30am looking to see if she was around. As I awaken that morning, there are several text messages with threats. **Can you say knocked off balance!** I am being stalked and threatened.

Not sure what she was capable of, I called the police. When they arrived, I'd tell the officer about the stalking and threats. He asked me what do I want to do and I said, *"Just talk to her and tell her to leave me alone."* He did, and she sent me a text later saying, *"You didn't have to call the police on me."* *"I just wanted to talk to you,"* she said. I said, *"I was on a date."* She replied, *"I thought you didn't want a relationship."* I said, *"I don't."* *"I'm confused, but I'll leave you alone,"* she said.

I mistreated and avoided this young lady because I didn't want to tell her the truth about dating other women. Ignoring her caused anger. When I told her that I didn't want a relationship, I also should have said that I will be dating others. I misled her with my actions. The problem was my mannerisms and treatment of the women I dated was confusing. She thought that I was only seeing her at the time. Following this encounter, I ensured myself that I would be crystal clear with my intentions on dating. **Can you relate?** That young lady and I would talk months later and apologize to each other. Today, we are friends and she has gotten married.

My current girlfriend reminds me of how fortunate I have been. She uses the word *"sampler"* to describe my previous encounters. She states that she was very hesitant to get involved with me. She'd ask a lot of probing questions related to sexual health. I'd assure her there's no STD's. Although she had only been divorced for several months, she would inform me that she is looking for something that would lead to a relationship. Tired of the same old patterns, deceit, and let downs that I've created, I thought that maybe it's time to give it a try.

Today, many of us are struggling to find a good mate. There are multiple reasons for the struggle. For some, fear, previous scars from past relationships, confusion about one's *identity, sexual preference,* bad advice from our friends, not looking for anyone, waiting for your knight in shining armor, *spirituality or lack thereof,* etc., tends to hinder that search. For those reasons, many people are free-lancing or "sampling" with no goal in sight.

In some socio-economic groups, men and women have allowed *sex or being sexy, materialism, TV shows and movies, social media*, and *stereo-types,* fool them on what they need to find or catch a good mate. They start going to desperate measures to impress or to be seen. Quick sexual encounters would arise from these encounters. You know what I'm speaking of. Women understand that a large percentage of the men are very visual creatures. So, they are spending any extra money they have on sexy clothes and heels, hair extensions, colored eye contacts, manicures/pedicures, body enhancements, tattoos etc. All these changes just to be noticed. Men are doing some very similar things: well-groomed hair (braids, beards, or bald), designer clothing and shoes, jewelry, expensive cars, tattoos. Where's the pride? *"Do not let your adorning be external, the braiding of hair and the putting on of gold jewelry, or the clothing you wear-but let your adorning be the hidden person of the heart with the imperishable beauty of a gentle and quiet spirit, which in God's sight is very precious." (1 Peter 3:3-4).*

Why are our standards so low? At the end of the day, is the impressive look even worth it? Is the image you're attractive to what you really want in a mate? How important will that image be ten, twenty, or thirty years from now? I'm sure there are some people whose impressive behaviors have captured the attention of their love and the relationships have led to the ultimate goal. I had a female friend who had invested a lot of time and money, endured a lot of stress and anxiety all just to impress and capture someone's attention. She would meet a handsome, single, financially stable man and they would date for a little while. Then he would inform her that he was attracted to her at first but then realized that this is not the kind of woman that he wants to move forward with. When she asked what you want, he replied, "a more natural woman." Can you say, **Knocked off-balance**! Was this guy serious about what he wanted or was he just a "sampler."

Now, I had the same mentality as this man. On impulse, I'm attracted to that sexy look as well but more of the classy and natural type. I would shy away from the made-up kind. Four years ago, an attractive, young lady who was shopping at a Target store in Raleigh, NC caught my attention. I would speak very friendly in a flirtatious way and she responded. She had long, straight hair, nice fitting jeans, nice pair of heels, and a sexy walk. We would talk briefly and exchange phone numbers. We'd meet a few days later for lunch. She would see me getting out of my Nissan Titan truck with khaki pants and a polo shirt on. She is looking very much like the day I met her. I'd give her compliments on how nice she looks.

After lunch, she invited me over to her home. I wasn't aware that her kids were there. She had a nineteen-year-old son and a six-year-old daughter who had ADHD. She would introduce me to both. The daughter didn't seem to be shy towards me. She was bringing over a game for me to play with her. Feeling a little uncomfortable, I would make up an excuse to leave. Later that evening, we would talk on the phone. She would ask me if I had another vehicle, do I often wear khakis and polos, and do I have any tattoos. I guess these were normal questions, right. A few days later, she would call and inform me that I was not her type and I didn't have any *"swag."* I think it was good that I didn't, and I wasn't going to change who I was to impress someone.

I was a little reluctant to put this chapter in the book. As I was writing mom's journey, I realized that she gave up on relationships in her early 50's. It wasn't that she was no longer attractive because she was still a beautiful woman. She was tired mentally and physically. She didn't need anyone who fed her constant lies, exhibiting jealousy, come home in a drunken state, and lash out at her because of her past. She wanted to be loved and appreciated, taken out on dates, but she wasn't getting that. So, she gave up on finding her prince charming. It wasn't that she lost the desire, but if one was not going to court and appreciate her, she would do without. Wow! Can you relate?

After mom was abandoned by her husband, she was trying to survive. That survival came with a lot of ungodly behaviors. Single men were not trying to commit to a relationship with mom. They were afraid of all the baggage or potentially taking care of all her kids. Nevertheless, they were interested in her body and her beauty. Several married men couldn't resist the temptations of mom's beauty and would offer money and or other help with no strings attached. Of course, one would lie and lead her on for years as long as he could get what he wanted. Then he'd look for a way to escape when mom applied pressure. *"No one who practices deceit shall dwell in my house; no one who utters lies shall continue before my eyes." (Psalm 101:7).*

I'm not sure how hurt mom was following the break up from my dad-the one who had his own construction business. She knew that the relationship was wrong anyway but she felt safe and appreciated by him. Although she felt safe, the relationship was dangerous. He was married and still lived with his wife. His wife knew what was going on. No one knew if she was plotting anything or not. She may have given her husband a threat or an ultimatum. They were both out of order and disobedient to God. She prayed and asked for forgiveness. Nevertheless, there's now three kids.

In this day and time, do you feel as though being yourself is too old-fashion. Can people still be attractive without all the extras? Will your mate accept you as you are despite your past and your current flaws? Are fairy tale encounters possible or just a hopeless imagination? Can you meet the potential soul mate in the mall, gym, church, school function, or work? Is it ok to pray for what or who you want? What about asking for guidance and direction when necessary! You may not always be given the right advice by friends and or family members, but God will not forsake you. You must trust and follow his lead. *"Ask, and it will be given to you; seek and you will find; knock, and it will be opened for you." (Matthew 7:7).*

What are we teaching our kids about relationships today? Are we letting TV, social media, and their friends guide them to what they feel a relationship looks like? What type of relationship are you seeking? Have you informed your friend or partner of your intentions? If your ultimate goal is marriage, is the person you're currently in a relationship with marriage material or have the same goal? If not, why waste your time for something that has no future. We all should use clarity with our expectations when we're seeking a relationship. Create transparency so that each understand what you are doing! If you are looking for something that will lead to the ultimate goal, be yourself. Fall in love because you enjoy each other's company, you're always thinking about the other, can't wait to see you, you're making each other smile often, etc. Love is emotions, sharing, caring, enjoying, supporting, comforting, protecting, etc.- not materialism.

Chapter 5

Marriage- Pretentious, Showy, Premature, Deceived, True love, American Dream

I didn't know Mr. Scott very well, but he struck me as a selfish, ungrounded young man. He was tickled that he had captured one of the most beautiful, young women in the neighborhood. His cousins and friends could now only drool. He wasn't patient enough to enjoy and appreciate mom. Marriage was not his **ultimate goal,** but he could not let mom get away and possibly marry his cousin or another man.

Marriage," The state of being united as spouses in consensual and contractual relationship by law." (Webster-Merriam.com).

As you prepared to go to the altar, did you and your spouse to be write your own vows or just go with the traditional ones. *"I take you to for my lawful spouse, to have and to hold from this day forward, for better or worse, in sickness and in health, until death do us part, I take you to be my spouse."* (theknot.com). Whether traditional or individually written, how sincere and genuine were you with your vows? Because the traditional marriage vows were written so long ago, do you realize how vague they are? It leaves out a whole lot of things that can be misunderstood. After reading my mom's story, take a minute to think about your marriage vows again now that you are married or about to be married! What would you want it to read?

Pretentious, Showy, Premature

Mr. Scott understood what he was doing. So, he married mom. I don't believe he was in love with her. *"For husbands, this means love your wives, just as Christ loved the church." (Ephesians 5:25).* He was very excited but not in love. If mom hadn't relayed her goal, he wouldn't have married her which would have been her gain. Instead, he would become a pretentious husband. He would work and sometimes take her out to a drive-in movie. When the kids started coming, he'd go out and buy milk, food, and clothing but didn't stay around long to help mom. He'd later say to his mother that, "I didn't really want to get married. I was too young and felt I was missing out on something." Have you heard this before?

Let's visit the story of Prince Charming for a minute! Do you recall reading the fairy tale books about Prince Charming rescuing a damsel in distress? The story would portray him as one of the most handsome and courageous man that a woman would ever meet. He's their savior and their protector. He was the ideal type of husband for young women. Although little girls fantasize on finding their Prince Charming, they are not as fortunate as Meghan Markle. **What does he look like in real life today?** How about the little boys? As we read the same fairy tale books, we would fantasize on marrying a princess. She would be beautiful, classy, rich, and the daughter of the king and queen. She would be very prissy, talk very proper, and have great mannerisms. **Guys, is this what you have today?** Think about it for a few moments!

Although those were fairy tale stories, they would give us the framework of what a great future partner looks like. Of course, they all may not have the perks of Prince Charming or a Princess; but, they could be molded just for you. Now, the fairy tale stories didn't want to frighten the kids, so they'd use frogs as a disguise for trickery. **At least that's how I saw it**. I'd imagine my mom looking at two frogs in the pond and one was a loud toad frog who'd wink at her while the other was a green frog(shy) who just stared. Of course, she would pick the winking toad frog from the pond, kiss him, and he would turn into her prince. Later, she'd realize that she had been tricked. Mr. Scott was not a prince at all, he was only a loud *"croaking frog."* Unfortunately, the green frog had hopped away and found another pond.

Don't get me wrong, my dad, the boyfriend of five years, was a frog too. Because he was a little larger in stature, we're going to label him as a *"bullfrog."* He'd hop into my mom's life at a very vulnerable state and charm her with kindness and **generosity**. Then, he would pretend to do things that he really couldn't produce. Later, exaggerate a misunderstood pregnancy diagnosis as an excuse to leap back into the pond. He would come by from time to time to see if his **"tadpoles"** were swimming but wouldn't offer them any direction. Wow! Can you relate? Is this still occurring today?

Do you know friends or family members who decided to get married because they wanted to show-off? They wanted a lavish ceremony better than yours, other family members, or their friend's wedding? *"A pretentious, showy life is an empty life; a plain and simple life is a full life." (Proverbs 13:7)*. Yet, they couldn't afford it and now they're in **debt**. Furthermore, they were not ready to get married. Now, the marriage becomes short-lived. Oftentimes, couples marry prematurely just to keep the other from getting away. Hmmm…. Do you know what I mean? Eventually, some fall in love after the fact and live happily ever after. Others struggle with the marriage and later divorce due to irreconcilable differences in a short period of time.

Do you believe that some people marry too young? I don't necessarily believe that. What I do believe is that couples should be ready to get married and not rush into it. If both come from families where they had watched their parents interact with love and realize that this is the kind of relationship they want as well, maybe they are ready regardless of the age.

Both are spiritually grounded and know that they will be committed to each other. Also, I believe that couples should read and understand their marriage vows before going to the altar.

Deceived

Abstaining from sex until marriage supposed to be a sign of sexual purity for both partners. *"For this is the will of God, your sanctification: that you abstain from sexual immorality; that each one of you know how to control his own body in holiness and honor." (Thessalonians 4:3-4).* If both partners agree to this commitment, there shouldn't be a problem, right. The fundamental reason for getting married should be that you're just in love, right. Although a good sexual relationship makes us feel special, happy, comfortable, confidence, and desired, and relieved, it should not be the basis for getting married. Usually, it's starts with the physical attraction, conversations, caring for, enjoying each other's company, and just the plain old getting to know each other. Mom had all those intangibles plus, she was ready for a sexual relationship. Wow! That sounds exciting, right. On the other hand, that relationship was going to come after she was married. Why is this so difficult to do nowadays?

Comedian Joy Behar recently joked that *"abstinence is what you do after you've been married for a long time."*

Although sexual intercourse declines in couples as they age, some still have the desire to be wanted. This brings me to the subject of *intimacy*. Can couples be intimate without engaging in sexual intercourse? Absolutely! All those fundamental reasons to fall in love, should lead to intimacy. It gives you a feeling of comfort and support without the stress and anxiety. You start to realize that when sexual intercourse occurs, it should be a relaxed and genuine feeling that may enhance the relationship even more. Of course, for many of us, *we can't wait to get it on*.

Many couples who are committing to abstinence before marriage, but some are becoming too impatient. They decide to get married too quickly just to have sex. Many have not gotten a chance to know each other well. The lack of communication on likes/dislikes, medical or sexual issues, and other things are not discussed yet. *Is it important to you to have complete transparency before marriage?* With their limelight careers, we can applaud football star Russell Wilson and singer Ciara, actress Meagan Good and her minister husband for their decision to remain abstinent before marriage. It's a major decision for anyone yet they pulled it off. Of course, there was great communication, patience, and faith.

Here's a story of a friend of mine and her husband to be! They had been dating for only a few months and decided to remain abstinent until marriage. They had met and fell for each other based on attraction, position, education, common spiritual beliefs, and financial status. The husband to be was heavily involved in the church-so he said. Plus, he was doing well financially. Both had been married before and each had kids from those marriages. They lived in different states-over 600 miles apart. As they took turns visiting each other, there were several red flags. Ex's were calling often, multiple prescription medicine bottles were on the table, husband to be didn't want to attend his church with the wife to be, and both seemed anxious from time to time. Nothing to worry about, right.

The husband to be persuaded his fiancé' to quit her job and move in with him. Excited to be married, they would plan a large, lavish, fairy-tale wedding. It was going to be like no others. Family and friends were astonished with the arrangements. There would be a lot of special songs sang before the vows were spoken. They have spoken their vows and are now husband and wife. A lavish reception and pictures would follow. The newlyweds can't wait to get to their hotel room and then start their honeymoon. The abstinence is about to be **overrrrrr.........**

The couple gets to the hotel room, skips the foreplay, and takes off all their clothes. It's about to be on and popping.

Uh oh, the husband can't get it up. Hmmm…. No problem! Some oral stimulation should help but no luck. *"Maybe there was just too much excitement and we both are tired and need to relax"*, she would say. She'd continue to say, *"when we get to our honeymoon destination, we're be ready."* Unfortunately, he would not be able to perform the entire honeymoon. Wow! All the excited is shattered. Later, he would inform her that he had an injury a few years back and it caused some damage to his genital area. Furthermore, he was taking medicine to help improve his issue, but it wasn't working. He is aroused occasionally but for the most part, he is ***impotent***. Can you say ***knocked off balance!*** What should happen next?

The wife felt as though she had been ***deceived*** and wasn't sure if she would continue with the marriage. She couldn't believe that her husband would conceal such an integral feature of their marriage. She would ask him to seek more medical help, but he'd say that he has done that for the past year. Also, she would ask him, "why didn't you tell me about your issue before we had gotten marry." He'd say, "why should that be such a big issue if we love each other." She would pray about it over the next few weeks. He would buy her very expensive items to hopefully ease the tension. He knows she is contemplating on leaving him so he's trying to buy her. Unfortunately, the money and gifts are not bringing her happiness.

Three months later, she would have the marriage *annulled* on the grounds of *concealment and impotency*. They would go their separate ways and remain friends. There would be no property to divide. She would use some of the finances from the sale of her home and business to rent an apartment and remove his name from the all business transactions. Currently, she is not dating or looking for anyone. She's learned some valuable lessons and has forgiven him. She's taking care of her kids and praying every day.

I have another female friend who states that she's been *celibate* for over 20 years. She is a very spiritual person, but she is waiting for her prince charming. She is a beautiful woman and has no trouble attracting men, but she wants someone who's grounded with the same spiritual beliefs. I've heard her joking with friends who are married to have an extra orgasm for her. Hmmm.... Apparently, she can't wait and it's obvious she desires that release. When that special guy comes along, will she ask him all about his sexual health, stamina, and endurance before taking that leap of faith?

True Love

Have you ever observed an older, married couple in church, in the stores, or anywhere else and say how happy, beautiful, loving, and precious they look? You say to yourself, that is true love. Some of them may be your siblings, parents, grandparents, etc. You may know or heard of their journey. Oftentimes, we hear or read about couples who have 40, 50, 60, or 75 years of marriages and we are in just astonished. How are they able to stay with each other for so long? What is the key to their long marriage? Are they honoring their vows until death due them part? Some of them are honoring their vows but others would say they're still in love.

Earlier this year, I was talking to one of my sisters and I asked her how long have you and Charles been married now. She replied, "forty-one years." Although I knew it had been a long time, it didn't dawn on me that it's been that long. She had one child before marriage and they have 4 children together. I applauded her for such a long marriage. She would say that it hasn't been easy, but they have overcome a lot of hurdles. Some *alcohol abuse* was one of the biggest issues in the marriage. Charles would have too many drinks and act out causing turmoil in the marriage. She would state that their involvement in the church has helped guide them through challenges. She'd also say how mom was her confidant and would always have encouraging words for her during difficult times.

Unlike many long-lasting marriages that began as love

at first sight, my sister and her husband had a different way of falling in love. You see, Charles was **blind** before they'd marry. They knew each other as kids but he lost his eyesight permanently before the age of 12. (**Determined course of life**). Of course, he'd recall that all the Scott girls were beautiful when he could see, and he knew he had a **"dime piece."** Their love for each other would grow from sharing, caring, and enjoying each other's presence. Although Charles was blind, he was a talented musician. He could play the piano and organ like no other in the state of NC. On top of that, he could sing just as well. Do you remember that song that was sung at mom's funeral? Yes, that was Charles. His performances would mesmerize crowds.

Unfortunately, his family didn't have the resources to send him to larger venues where his talents could be discovered. This was one of the reasons for his alcohol abuse. He would perform at events and churches all over the sandhills region. He was a one man show and didn't need any help performing. My sister would be there supporting him 100%. Later in their marriage, my sister, Diane, would become a school teacher. This seem to be her calling. She always had the patience and ability to get your attention. I recall how she'd help teach me and the other two youngest brothers how to read. She'd be able to bring imagination into our reading which enhanced our focus. She'd apply those same techniques with her husband and kids. Most of us would go on to become good readers, spelling bee champions, teacher's pets, etc. all through grammar school. For some, we'd carry that same ability into our college education. *Smile sister, more than you realize was attributed to you!*

As she told me earlier, her marriage has been no different than others. There have been many challenges. Sometimes, after drinking, Charles would act out so to speak. He'd want to flirt with women in his presence. He'd ask for hugs and feel their arms since he couldn't see them! My sister would get angry of course. Also, he'd have moments of envy towards other local musicians who seem to have much less talent than he had but are making more money. He'd wonder how things would be if he could see, work, and travel to perform. *"Beyond your abilities, God has you right where he wants you to be." (RickThomas.net).*

What if Charles had the abilities that he imagined, he may not have the blessings or people in his life. His course of life could be better or worse. Would it be worth the risk? He'd realize that he has a wonderful wife and a beautiful family who loves him unconditionally. His amazing wife, my sister, has stood by his side throughout all his pain and imperfections. I don't believe for a minute that he would ever want to change that. *"But when the perfect comes, the partial will be done away." (Corinthians 13:10).* Furthermore, he is following the work of the Lord.   Many others in your line of work are not on that path. Can you relate?

American Dream

I got married at the age of 24. Not as young as mom and her husband but we're now in a different era and lifestyle! I had graduated from college and had an entry level retail management job. Things were on the up and up. My wife and I had dated off and on for 5 years prior to marriage. She was a pretty, little thing who caught my attention at a sorority party. She didn't seem too interested in me at first. See, I was a handsome, yet a skinny young man with a lot of **acne (Physical Appearance)** on my face. The blackheads on a light complexion face appeared to look green. Plus, an occasional large pimple would erupt in the worst spot. She didn't know what to think. Can you relate? Nevertheless, I'd continue to pursue her, and we eventually started dating.

She was on the track team in college and I was on the men's basketball team. She was a local girl with a car and would pick me up for a movie, shopping, dinner, etc. Coming from a poor family, I never had any money, but she understood and didn't mind paying for things. She was a very nice, supportive young lady with good family values. In the winter of my freshman year, I had injured my right ankle and it required *surgery*. She was right by my side through the whole ordeal. She grew up in the *church* and was still active. She had an older brother in the military and a younger sister in middle school. Her mom and dad had divorced 5 years prior to us meeting yet they were very active in their kid's lives. Both of her parents would advise her on meeting guys with potential to be a husband and not one's who just want to sleep around. Although I didn't come from a great family structure, I recalled my mom telling me that, *"you'll be a great husband one day because you listen, show appreciation, and pay attention."* Although I remember and appreciated her words, I didn't think much of that statement then because I was young and not even thinking of marriage. My future wife would see those actions first-hand.

For the remainder of my freshman year, I'd have bouts of anxiety because of my ankle injury. I felt neglected by the coaching staff following the injury. My girlfriend would tell me to hang in there, it'll get better. So, I began to work out religiously. Because of my body structure, I'd eat to gain weight and work out to burn the calories. That fall, I'd enter my red-shirt freshman year 22lbs heavier, buffed, tan, and in good physical shape. I did this for myself because I wanted to be ready for basketball. It paid off because I was the starter at shooting guard when the season began. The bad thing for my future wife was that I garnered a lot of attention from the young ladies on campus. They would flirt relentlessly. **Peer pressure** and not being grounded would lead me to pursue some of these young ladies even though it was not what I really wanted. I would be honest with my future wife and let her know that I got overwhelmed and realized that maybe I'm not ready for anything serious yet. Hurt, she asked, *"what do you want us to do?"* I replied, *"I don't know but I don't want to lose you."* She'd hang in there with me but would go on occasional dates with someone else. She was allowing me to "sow my oats."

What makes us become so selfish? Oftentimes, we know what we want, but temptations and weakness steps in and we don't have the will power to fight it off. Then, we end up losing the best thing for us. Can you relate? The next year, my future wife is pregnant with our first child. Upset and not ready to be a father, I questioned her about birth control pills because I thought she was taking them. Then I realized that I was irresponsible as well. The pregnancy would **knock both of us off-balance (Unplanned Parenthood)**. Her course of life would be changed more than mine. Although we were both still in college, she'd have to take some time off. Even though her parents didn't condone kids born out of wedlock, neither of us believed in abortions so Clay Jr would be born in August of 1989. We didn't allow the birth of our first child to force us to marry. We would continue to date and grow into the relationship. There would be some rough patches before we'd marry but we still knew we were the ones for each other. We would write our own vows and get married in 1992.

The first years of our marriage would be typical. I had landed a better job with good pay and even better benefits. We would purchase our first house in the suburbs of Nashville and buy a new car. There was a lot of excitement. We would go on family vacations, attend church, visit family in NC, and participate in neighborhood events. We would have social gatherings at our house or at friend's and family's houses. *My mom envisioned this kind of life too*. Our marriage was going well. My wife would enter nursing school and work part time. While she was in school, we would have our second child. A year and a half later, she'd graduate from Belmont University School of Nursing. Our third and final child would be born that following spring. She had worked part-time at Vanderbilt Medical Center and upon graduation, they would hire her as a nurse in the ER. She was excited about being a nurse and helping people. It was also gratifying that our income would almost double.

We have now established ourselves as a good church going, middle-income, educated family with little debt, high credit scores, and respected in the neighborhood. Our life is well balanced. I had begun my baseball coaching career and had become very respected for my knowledge of the game. Other coaches and parents had encouraged me to be a board member. My wife is inputting on a lot of fundraising ideas and is well-liked by the parents as well. ***We have become grounded and living the "American Dream", right.***

Over the next 10 years, the marriage would remain stable. We would have normal disagreements but nothing significant. We'd move back into East Nashville where my wife grew up. The kids (3 boys) are growing up, doing well in school, boy scouts, and sports. The 3 boys and myself would get baptized at church and start attending some ministries. We are now well established in the community, involved in church, neighborhood, gyms, and baseball fields. I am continuing my coaching of baseball and basketball. My wife is the team mom of all my teams. She is excited to take on the role. Her support of me and the kids is outstanding. The moms and dads of our players are ecstatic to be a part of our teams. Our friends and families are portraying us as the model family.

Our boys would begin to play football too. Now, there are sports all year-round in the Scott house. Although I'm not coaching football, we are very involved with fundraising, etc. Every weekend, we're tied up with sports activities. When my wife and I had free time, we were often too exhausted from sports and work to do much together. As time progressed, some frustrations would set in. Arguments would increase. My grandmother had told mom that there be days like this. Often, we would let the disagreements subside without reaching a resolution or compromise. We are slowly losing our **balance**. We were allowing little things to cause future problems and didn't realize they could potentially damage our marriage. *"Examine yourselves, to see whether you are in the faith. Test yourselves. Or do you not realize this about yourselves, that Jesus Christ is in you? Unless indeed you fail to meet the test!"* (*2 Corinthian 13:5*). Speaking for myself, I was physically exhausted at times and I was allowing it to cloud my judgements, communication, and decision making. Both of us had gotten **off balance** and were not examining the issues thoroughly. Our test scores were at the **"D"** level and we didn't realize it.

What are you doing to stay on course? Which marriage category are you in? Are you honoring your marriage vows and following God's course? Are you praying for your marriage? Are you resolving all conflicts? Are you making some changes or improvements in your marriage? Or, are you accepting things the way they are, and hoping they resolve on their own?

Chapter 6

Tell Tale Signs Leading to Divorce

Many people would think that the number one cause of divorce is **Infidelity**. Little do we realize it, **communication** is the primary reason. The failure to communicate usually leads to multiple issues in the marriage*. (Polled by Huffington Post).* The deceived couple who practiced abstinence before marriage was a good example of poor communication. They both ignored the red flags and chose not to discuss them.

Were Mr. Scott's flirtatious ways a sign that could lead to marital issues? Did mom think that would change or go away as the marriage progressed? The answers to both questions are probably a "Yes." Never did mom imagine that her marriage would be over after fifteen years and twelve kids, but it was. Because Mr. Scott left her and never came back, there was no final divorce. I'm not sure what grounds for divorce would have applied. Was it abandonment, infidelity, mental abuse, or just irreconcilable differences? Either way, it was not your typical separation or divorce. **What were your reasons? Did it knock you off balance? Was it a sigh of relief? Are you happy now or still feeling the pain?**

My marriage demise was a prime example of miscommunication or lack thereof which led to other issues. I want my story to help other couples realize that you should never take your marriage for granted. Marriage is work. No one ever said that it would be easy, but it shouldn't be that hard either. We allowed our perceptions of what should be occurring in the marriage drive us to our pitfalls. Also, we let our **wants and desires** over-shadow our needs, self-control, and love for each other. When that happened, Satan, with his deception, stepped in and stirred the pot." *Do not deprive each other except perhaps by mutual consent and for a time, so that you may devote yourselves to prayer. Then come together again so that Satan will not tempt you because of your lack of self-control." (1 Corinthians 7:5).* Although we were going to church, we were not praying and we didn't have God in our lives. Divorce should have never been on the radar.

Here's my story!

In the summer of 2000, I had a **vasectomy**. Three kids were enough, so I thought. My wife was tired of all forms of birth control. We would briefly discuss a hysterectomy, but she'd defer to me. So, I decided to proceed. It took me a while to get over the fear but after collaborating with friends who had the procedure and my Urologist, I manned up. A year later, my wife was feeling that I moved too quickly on having the procedure. She'd say that we didn't discuss it thoroughly. She would say that we never really said that we were done with kids. We were only thirty-two and thirty-three years old. Can you say, "Be Clear on your communication!"

In early 2002, my wife ran across an old psychology professor from college. He was from Nigeria and I recalled my wife talking about not understanding him when he was teaching class due to his accent. She'd wait till the end of class to get clarity on the assignments. Anyway, he was working at Vanderbilt Medical Center as a child psychiatrist. She would talk to him regularly after work. It was nothing for me to be alarmed about. There was no jealousy or insecurities in our marriage. Suddenly, my wife would come home very horny and was ready to get it on. **Whoopeee!!!!** I liked that, and I was excited every time. It felt good that she was wanting me like that. See, I had some on and off struggles with *Erectile Dysfunction* and it caused a lot of *anxiety* in my sex life. During this time, there were no *ED* problems. Maybe it was being desired every night that kept me aroused. I wasn't sure what her and the doctor were doing or talking about, but it was working, and I wasn't curious about anything, at least not yet.

A month later, calls from VUMC would come to the house phone. When I'd answer, the person would hang up. One night, the person would ask for my wife and it sounded like a person with an African accent. I'd ask if I could take a message and he says I'll call back another time. See, my wife didn't have a cell phone yet. When I asked her why would the doctor be calling the house, she'd say I don't know, she didn't give him our number. I asked her to find out if it was him. I'd go on to ask if there was something else going on with the two of you. She'd reply, "no, we have only been discussing our oldest son's behavior issues." I replied, "if this is him calling the house, then I have a problem with that; furthermore, why are you all discussing our son's behavior when there's no current issues with him." If so, why don't we take our son to talk with him together since he's a child psychiatrist. *"Do not lie to one another, seeing that you have put off the old self with its practices." (Colossians 3:9).*

Our son, thirteen at the time, was expelled from summer camp because he and a young lady were caught in a bathroom stall together. They were thinking of doing something, but nothing happened yet. Nevertheless, my wife would cut off the communication with the doctor and the excitement would seize. The abrupt change in her behavior now had me wondering if there was more to their communication. Not only had her desire to have sex frequently changed, we were not having sex hardly at all. She had made me feel as though I've done something wrong. Now, my **anxiety** has triggered the **erectile dysfunction** again. I don't think either of us paid attention to this occurrence and potential

79

contributing factor.

A year later, my mom would become very ill and I'm traveling to NC to see her. I had met a beautiful woman a few months prior at my son's school while doing Parent Patrol. We'd have small chats at school then exchange phone numbers. Well, one night on my way to Charlotte, NC to see mom, the beautiful woman asked to see me. She would offer me the **Presidential cigar special** before I hit the road. "Something to smile about on the way," she said. I knew it was wrong, but I wasn't getting it at home. I had a moment of being desired again. *"The righteousness of the upright delivers them, but the unfaithful are trapped by evil desires." (Proverbs 11:6).* This woman was married too but her husband was **incarcerated** at the time. I'd have more chats with the woman and we'd engage in sexual intercourse one afternoon, but we didn't take things any further. There probably would have been more engagements but her husband was being released. I don't think my wife knew and I never told her.

There had been two other attempted sexual encounters by me earlier in our marriage. Unfortunately, they'd both be interrupted by ED. They were embarrassing but both times they were nervous and over anxious moments. Both encounters were with married women. They were having trouble in their marriage and needing a release. Whew!! As I thought about it later, it's good that it didn't happen. Once again, I knew it was wrong. I was caught up in the moment. I would have other flirtatious encounters while hanging out with friends but wouldn't pursue anything. It was somewhat exciting listening to friends tell of their escapades and embellishments. Oftentimes, I feel the urge to do the same, but I preferred that my friends knew nothing about my transgressions. Although there were opportunities for other affairs, I knew it was wrong. I was afraid of how easy it was; plus, I had my anxiety about ED. Maybe it was just a sign from God that I shouldn't have this **lust** and desires anyway.

As time passed, we'd have arguments over home repairs, kid's college funds, NC family visits, etc. Our visits to NC would change after mom passed. My wife wasn't too excited to go there anymore but went anyway. I'd mention to her that I have no problem with her staying at home. She'd talk about her supporting me with things such as family visits and sports, but it wasn't reciprocated. Keep in mind, most of my family is in NC while all her family is here in Nashville. We could visit her family anytime, but she chose not to. There was one evening that some of her family gathered at her grandmother's house a week after her grandmother passed away. I wasn't quite sure if she wanted me to go or not because we had gathered for a little while following the funeral. So, I didn't go. I felt bad about it

later when she came home, but I couldn't change it now.
Nevertheless, I would always support her with other events and
her marathon races as well. Me and the boys would drive her to
the marathons and make signs to show our support.

In the winter of 2004, I'd receive emails from friends in
NC about joining **Facebook** to connect with others that I hadn't
talked to in a while. I told my wife about the social media site
and she was not fond of it at all. She'd ask me why was I trying
to connect with others as though it was for other reasons. I'd
assure her that the connection had nothing to do with seeing
someone. She wouldn't comment anymore; so, we left it alone.
I would only reach out to class members for our upcoming 2006
class reunion. Because I saw the social media thing as a
potential problem for us, I wouldn't get on the site anymore
while we were married.

Nevertheless, she was still bothered by the ordeal. We
would continue to argue about so many little things and I didn't
understand why they were such a big problem. We were
needing prayer and or counseling. I needed to understand what
is really affecting our marriage because something is missing.
Although we were attending church, we were not spiritually
grounded like we needed to be, and we were not interested in
having the church minister help us either. So, we would both
agree to get some *marriage counseling* to help us improve our

situations. *"Listen to advice and accept instruction, that you may gain wisdom in the future." (Proverbs 19:20).* Plus, I'd seek medical attention for my **ED**. These issues seem correctable, right.

While in counseling, she'd tell me that I've taken her for granted, don't compliment her, don't introduce her to my friends, and don't appreciate her. Furthermore, she'd tell me I'm **selfish**. She referenced her sexual frustration because of my ED but stated that she could deal with it if other items were improved. While in the session, I asked her why she wasn't saying something about her feelings when the events were happening (such as taking her for granted, introductions) and she said that I should have known. *Draw things to each other's attention and let them know how it affects you! Most of us, do not want to keep making the same mistakes. Do we always know what to do in a marriage? Are you communicating your feelings of displeasure when it occurs or allowing them to alter your thoughts? Do you believe in* **Satan's deception**? He steps in when we're least expecting.

I would begin to work on all these things. Counseling is going pretty well, so I thought. Nevertheless, I don't think it mattered so much to my wife now. She felt unappreciated and unprotected. In a good marriage, men and women should make each other feel a sense of worth. It's a wonderful feeling to know that your spouse appreciates everything you do for them. My behaviors had given **Satan** a window of opportunity. He would tell my wife that I don't deserve her and don't treat her like the queen that she is. He would say that he doesn't want you to be **submissive** to him because he is not covering you. Instead, he wants to control and make his own rules.

In the early fall of 2006, we were invited to a friend's house party. He and his wife were celebrating the pregnancy of triplets. My wife was tired from a day of football with our kids plus she was on call for work. So, I went alone. It was a good party with good food, music, friends, and conversations. There was drinking, cigar smoking *(tobacco this time)*, and flirting. About 1am, I began to feel a little queasy and stepped down from the deck in case I had to vomit. Not only did I vomit but I passed out too. The host of the party and friends picked me up and took me into the guest room with a towel in case of more vomiting. The next thing I know, I awaken at 7:45am. I have missed several calls from my wife. She is fretting that something has happened to me. Momentarily, she is **knocked off balance**. This type of occurrence had never happened in our marriage before.

I wake up the host to let me out of the house, so I don't set off the alarm. I ask him if anyone called my wife and he said,

"I don't think so." I get home a little after 8am and she asked, "what happened." She was very worried and about to call the police. I'd inform her that I got drunk and passed out at the host house. She asked why didn't someone call me. I replied, no one had the number without getting it out of my cell phone. I have allowed Satan to step in and cloud my judgement. He also used his deceptive ways to prevent my friends from finding a way to contact my wife and let her know my status. **Wow! Can you envision that!**

My wife didn't believe my story. She thought I was making it up to cover for *Infidelity*. I offered to call my friend to confirm my story, but she didn't want to do that either. I apologized and told her that it must have been the cigar that put me in such a state. See, I had only been drunk once prior and that was while in college nearly 20 years ago. That Trust was now broken, and it didn't matter what I said or done. It was going to take time for the healing. *"Trust is the bedrock of what makes relationships work. It's the fundamental process of love and intimacy." (5 Ways to Rebuild Trust After It's broken, by Dr. Bill Cloke).*

Our marriage would take a downward spiral from this point until the end. She would have dinner with an old male friend in November of the same year. She'd tell me before the fact, but it didn't matter what I thought. We'd argue about it a little yet reach no compromise or understanding. There would be distance in the house throughout the holidays. We'd continue counseling at the beginning of the year but now a new twist has arisen. My wife has befriended another man at the local YMCA that we attend as a family. The chats have grown into something more. I was hit with a left hook and didn't see it coming! I'd ask her, "do you realize that you're about to destroy this family?" She'd tell me that she didn't want our marriage to be over. She'd state that she felt desired and captivated by the flattery. Plus, he caught me at a vulnerable time, she'd say. *"Even Satan disguises himself as an angel of light. So, it is no surprise if his servants, also, disguise themselves as servants of righteousness." (Corinthians 11:14-15).* I'd tell her that's what men do when they are seeking out a woman, but you're married, and you should have said you're not available.

She would deny any sexual activity, yet all the signs were there. She would say, "it's over between her and her friend yet there was still contact. Now, my **trust** in her is shattered. I'm finding myself constantly looking for things, angry, and belligerent. The kids would hear us arguing constantly. The younger two would go to their rooms and close the doors. Sometimes, the older one would come to ensure we were not physically fighting. We are completely ***off-balance.***

Oftentimes, the younger boys would have homework questions or need help with something else but afraid to approach either of us-especially me because my demeanor had completely changed. We had become so engulfed with emotions that we didn't realize how we were neglecting our children. Fortunately, we had built a solid **foundational structure** well before all the problems erupted, so we thought. (See Matthew 7:24-27).

One year later, after struggling through the alleged affair, she would befriend another man. This guy was an umpire at the park where our kids played baseball. I felt as though I was a tomcat and she was dangling a mouse in my face. Her choice of clothes had changed as though she was trying to be sexier and it didn't appear she was doing it for me. We would discuss the friendship and the clothes, and she'd say that they just had lunch and the clothes were just something different. **Hmmm....** One thing that perturbed me the most was that, she never apologized for her actions. As though, it's was my previous actions that caused her to seek the attention.

Even though I didn't know my mom's full story at the time, there were similarities between the two of us. See, I didn't want to give up on our marriage because of the circumstances. *"Rejoice always, pray continually, give thanks in all circumstances; for this is God's will for you in Christ*

Jesus." (Thessalonians 5 16:18). Plus, I did realize that my actions or lack thereof contributed to some of my wife's behaviors. My mother allowed her husband to come back after nearly a year hiatus because she felt her actions were flawed. Plus, she still loved her husband despite his wrong doings. That was my feelings as well. I loved my wife but maybe my previous actions didn't show it. *"Love is patient, love is kind. It does not envy, it does not boast, it is not proud. It does not dishonor others, it is not self-seeking, it is not easily angered, it keeps no record of wrongs." (Corinthians 13:4-5)*.

Nevertheless, she was impatient with the changes following counseling and felt that I should have been exhibiting those positive behaviors long before her thoughts of **infidelity**. Furthermore, I'd think of the poor treatment I've exhibited to her over the years. Plus, recalling my moments of **infidelity** too. I'd also think about some of the NC visits. For years, I'd leave her and the kids at mom's house while I went to Walmart and or visit friends whom I hadn't seen in a while. Although she didn't seem to mind, it came up in marriage counseling. When it was occurring, I didn't think it was so bad, but I realized that I was leaving her **unprotected**. Not in a harmful way but leaving her feeling unimportant. After my brother El and mom passed, my wife wasn't left behind anymore. Nevertheless, the visits weren't the same. As you see, I wasn't a saint and didn't try to act as though I was.

Not wanting to give up on our marriage, I would do some self-healing while my wife would get some individual counseling. I would blame myself for her actions. I'd think of the drunken event and other unpleasant situations that I had put her in. We'd have moments of improvement over the next 3 years. We'd spend more time together, take in movies, and weekend trips. Nevertheless, we could never seem to jump that hurdle. One thing that we were not doing or at least I wasn't, is **praying** for our marriage. There was no **war room** set up neither mentally or physically. Our communication was more of talking at each other instead or working things out. The arguments would become a vicious circle. I would find out that she had opened a separate bank account without my knowledge in preparation of divorce. When I asked her about it, she said that "she had consulted with an attorney and that was one of the recommendations." Are we given up?

In the spring of 2010, I'd tell my wife that my company is putting me in an advanced leadership program to prepare me for the next level of management. It would require traveling one week out of each month for the next six months. I'd explain to her and the kids what I'm doing and the things I'm learning. She initially seemed excited for me but uninterested in hearing my stories. In October, a middle management job came open at work and my mentors thought I was the prime candidate for the position. Knowing that the job entailed 24-hour responsibility, replying to emails, and answering phone calls in the middle of the night, I turned it down because I realized that it was not the right time due to my marital problems.

Two months later, while sitting in the gym watching our youngest son's basketball game, a beautiful woman enters the gym with a large, manila envelope. I'm trying not to stare because my middle son is sitting beside me, and my wife is behind me. Well, she comes right up to me and ask, "are you Mr. Clayvon Scott?" I reply, "yes" and she hands me the envelope and walks away. Curious, I open the envelope and see **divorce** papers. Can you say **knocked off-balance**! I'd turn to my wife and shake my head. My son next to me ask, "Is everything ok dad?" I replied, "Yes" everything is ok. Just surprised!

This was a time that I could really use some help from mom, but she was already in heaven-watching us but unable to speak. Our marriage had been struggling for years and even though I realized it may come to this point, I was not going to be the one to file. Mom may have been able to guide us or me with some words of wisdom. She would have prayed for our marriage. I believe she would have reminded us that *"there be times like this that challenge us, but our faith in God is what helps us overcome."*

My wife and I would talk following the delivery and I asked, "Why do it in front of our kids?" She replied, "To ensure you got it." Wow! Really! Nevertheless, I asked, "is this what you really want?" She would reply, "I'm not happy, we're not getting anywhere." "I'm feeling as though I've never been in love with you, she'd reference her sexual frustrations, and neither of us is fighting for the marriage," she'd exclaim. **Wow!** I felt belittled and as though I never added up to her expectations. Following this conversation, I'm trying to figure everything out while keeping the kids at bay. It's become too miserable to stay in the house together. I informed my wife that I was moving out within six months.

On the day of the move, my wife asks me to come into the bedroom. She breaks down and cries. Then she says, "I can't believe this is happening." I replied, "isn't this what you wanted?" She says, "I wanted you to fight for me." Now, I'm confused. You want me to fight but you're unhappy, we're not progressing, you're not sure if you ever loved me, and you filed for divorce. I ask, "why did you wait until I was moving out to say anything." I go on to say that, "we're not divorced yet. Maybe we can try to talk, and go out sometimes to see what happens." *"Love never gives up; and its faith, hope, and patience never fail." (Corinthians 13:7).*

I thought my wife had given up. Threw in the towel! I had prepared myself for the end of the marriage. There were no signs of reconciling. Nothing was **communicated** to show in difference. We would talk briefly a couple times over the next month. I would invite her and the kids over to my apartment on Memorial Day for swimming and grilling. All would show up and we had a good day. She and I would mention a movie and dinner for another time, but it never happened. See, I am now enjoying the freedom, relaxation, and being desired by beautiful single women. Now, I am getting what I want without the stress and anxiety. *I'd later realize that, if my wife wanted to fight for us, then she should not have let me leave that house.*

There are consequences to every decision we make. They could be good or bad. Uncertainty, brings about a lot of anxiety. You start to second guess your decisions. Then you realize you've made the wrong decisions. A year later, we were getting a divorce after nearly 20 years of marriage. We were both too stubborn to put in the work to save our marriage. We did not **pray** for it. Our marriage vows had blown away with the wind. Communication had ceased the last three months prior to her filing for divorce. So, I took it that her mind was made up. She would be **controlled** no more. Or at least, I would not worry about telling her what we were not going to do anymore. See, the damage had changed me as a husband and I found myself constantly looking for things to ensure they weren't happening anymore.

It was a sad and happy day going into the final divorce. Both of us were ready for it to be over but I think neither of us were at peace with the decision. We would move on to a **new course of life** without each other. We would continue to take care of our parenting duties. But here is one thing that caught me **off guard**. Late April of this year, while leaving a birthday dinner for our youngest two boys, my ex and I would have a brief conversation outside of the restaurant. We would give each other a compliment, and ask how we're doing. I'd inform her that I am writing a book. She'd ask if it's about us. I'd tell her that there's a lot about us but more about family and friends too. She'd go on to ask, **"Do you think we should have gotten a divorce?"** Not wanting to say the wrong thing, I responded and said, "we were unhappy for a long time and we were not getting anywhere."

Take a moment to look at some of these marriage vows! Ask yourself, have I pledged any of these things to my spouse? Did I honor these vows before our demise? Did I allow Satan's deception to interfere? As my wife and I began to hit a different stage in our life, we lost focus of our marriage vows.

"I, _____ take you, _____ to be my husband/wife, to love and to hold from this day forward, for better or for worse, for

richer or for poorer, in sickness and in health, to love and to cherish until death do us part. This is my solemn vow."

" I pledge to share my life openly with you, to speak the truth to you in love; I promise to honor and tenderly care for you, to cherish and encourage your own fulfillment as an individual through all the changes of our lives."

"I pledge to support you, encourage you, guide you, trust you, protect you through all of our days."

"I pledge to be your friend and lover, companion and helper, so help me God."

" I promise to be faithful to you alone as long as we both shall live."

" I pledge to be the mother/father to your children, and the companion of my days. I promise to fully share my life with you, through days of happiness or sadness, abundance or want. I pledge to you my unfailing love always."
(From Reverend Beverly Fest, Mountain Ministry in Boulder, CO).

Here are a few more I added on the lines of **Submission**! Do you trust your spouse to be totally submissive? Oftentimes, it's misconstrued with **control**. I never meant for my behaviors to come across as controlling yet, I never really understood submission. Neither of you should have any worries. You are in a partnership, right. The wives are not the only ones who should be submissive. *"Submit to one another out of reverence for Christ." (Ephesians 5:21).*

"I pledge to be your eyes when you can't see, your voice when you can't talk, your ears when you can't hear, your legs when you can't walk."

"I pledge to comfort, nourish, and care for you when you're sick. To be your decision maker when your mind and or thoughts are altered."

We have been divorced for 5 years and I am finally finding some resolve to our demise. I have forgiven her and hopefully she has forgiven me as well. Although our kids are older, I have become a better father than I've ever been. I am giving them more love, support, guidance, encouragement, and inspiration. I have overcome past hang-ups and ready to share my story with others in hope of helping, healing, and forgiving. I'm praying more than ever while incorporating a scripture and a daily devotional every day. Thanks, Tony Dungy (Uncommon Life). I've learned from my mistakes in the marriage and don't plan to make those same mistakes again.

What is your current situation? Are you giving up on your marriage? Are you praying for it? Are you reaching out for guidance? Are you recalling and or honoring your marriage vows?

Chapter 7

Loneliness: Discontentment, Sadness, Empty Nester

Often when we're having relationship issues, we cut off communication with family and friends to work on those issues. At times, we'll consult with a counselor, minister, or just work it out on our own. When all else fails, the relationship ends. A short time later, we experience a period of sadness, pain, and unbalance. Others may experience joy and happiness. How do you recover? Are you lonely?

"Loneliness is defined as, sadness because one has no friends or company." (Merriam-Webster).

Discontentment

Mom had periods of loneliness because she was literally left alone. Even when Mr. Scott was home, there was emptiness. That's because he wasn't bringing much substance to the marriage. Either the make-up sex was the **Bomb** or mom just missed being held. Although mom continued to be desired my Mr. Scott, she could tell his actions were not genuine. He was hurting her emotionally all the time and didn't seem to care. Fortunately, she walked with God. *You could have people around you throughout the day or even be in a lifelong marriage, and still experience deep, pervasive loneliness. (psychologytoday.com).* I believe this is what my ex-wife was experiencing towards the end of our marriage. When she stated that I didn't compliment her, she felt as though I didn't see her. When I didn't introduce her to some of my friends in passing, she felt worthless and unappreciated. She stated that I didn't seem proud to have her as my wife. In a way, her feelings were an example of me leaving her unprotected and **Satan** was smiling. My current girlfriend told me that this was the same way she had felt in her marriage for years, but she ***prayed*** about it.

My actions or lack thereof had left my ex-wife feeling vulnerable and uncovered. Now, these statements from her came out during our marriage counseling prior to her infidelity and I realized that I had taken her for granted. Although I promised to work on these things, it was a little too late. She would feel as though my efforts were not genuine which still left her feeling lonely. That loneliness and ***discontentment*** would leave her emotionally off balance-eventually leading to an ***Affair***.

Prior to my ex-wife asking me, *"Do I think we should have gotten a divorce?"* She had reconnected with some of our old friends that she hadn't talked to in years. I'm assuming she started feeling a certain way after talking with them. See, she had totally disconnected herself from a lot of friends during our marital issues. I, on the other hand, would talk to them but seldom. They were aware of our marital problems and would offer help if needed. All our friends and family were shocked to hear of our divorce. They thought we were the picture-perfect family. Five years later, they'd realize that both of us are still single. Some would hint to me about us getting back together but I'd tell them that I'm in a different place now. If she hadn't been so bitter over the last five years, that could've been a consideration. It was just enlightening that we could talk following the dinner without un-pleasantry and confrontation. I'm more comfortable with us being friends because we still have young men to help guide.

Following our divorce, I would have some sad and happy days. It took me a while to start recovering from the divorce. I just couldn't believe that we let something so good deteriorate and lead to our demise. I was lonely but disguised it for a while. Yes, I was meeting some beautiful single women, but they could hear my pain. I would often have dinner and romantic times with some of them but never any emotional attachment. In fact, I was living a Rick James, **"Love them and leave them life."** That was not my claim to fame. I would hang out with them on Saturday and wouldn't talk to them again for a week. It wasn't that I was talking to someone else in between time; I just didn't want to be bothered.

Sadness

There are many different aspects of loneliness. One of the most common ones, is the death of a loved one. Not only did my mom experience loneliness in the marriage, she also experienced it when we lost our brother, El. From the time El went blind in 1984 until his death in 1997, mom took care of him. Their bond had grown stronger than any other sibling because of the constant care. The two of them were the only ones in the home from 1988-1997. When El passed away, she was left alone. Ell's death was two-fold for mom. Not only would she lose a child before her own death, she'd also lose the one that kept her strong and upright for years.   His ability to stay strong despite his challenges kept her strong too. She knew El was a special child and was going to a special place in heaven. For that reason, she kept her faith. *"For I consider that the sufferings of this present time are not worth comparing with the glory that is to be revealed to us."* *(Romans 8:18)*.

My brother, Steve, lost his wife in late 2008 due to a heart attack. They had been married for 28 years. Unquestionably, she was the love of his life. She would handle all the business affairs. The only thing Steve had to do was work, take care of outside chores, and occasionally cook. They didn't have any kids of their own, but they had 2 nephews and a niece move in with them at early ages. They would raise these kids until graduation of high school and off to college or the military. They would brag about the accomplishments of the kids and the kids were very appreciative, so it seemed.

When Steve's wife passed away, he was left alone. All the kids are grown and doing their own thing. They would come to the funeral but never came to check on Steve and or offer any assistance. He had become very distraught and lonely. He'd continue to work his M-F job but he's drinking heavily every weekend. Because his wife handled all the business affairs, family offered to help him with all his bill payments. He insisted on doing it himself. Concerned about his drinking and well-being, family would collaborate on finding a responsible and helpful family member to live with him. Unfortunately, we couldn't come up with one.

Steve would endure a lot more heart aches during the next 7 years. Other siblings very close to him would pass away. Family members would take advantage of his generosity while at such a vulnerable state. He would retire from his job in 2014. Although it was a momentous occasion for him, it was sad too because his wife was not around to help him enjoy his retirement. Today, Steve continues to struggle with loneliness. A couple of siblings have done an *intervention* to help monitor his drinking, rid his dwelling of vultures, and control his financial affairs. Occasionally, he attends family functions but has no desire to do much of anything else. Often when he's drinking, he likes to sing. His favorite song is "Three times a Lady" by The Commodores. I'm sure he is referencing his wife and our mom. He misses them dearly and miss talking to them. *"You never realize how lonely you are until it's the end of the day and you got a bunch of things to talk about and no one to talk to."* (*Relationship Rules*).

A dear friend of mine, Tonya, lost her son in the fall of 2012 at the age of twenty-five. After leaving the YMCA and crossing the street to walk home, he was struck by a car and killed. The vehicle never stopped, and she would find out later that it was a drunk driver. This unexpected event would knock her off balance and change her course of life. See, he was her only child and they were always doing things together. He was a very spiritual young man who helped her establish an organization called, "Children of the King." It was a non-profit organization that helped troubled, abandoned kids, homeless, and others find their way through Christ.

Tonya had long periods of loneliness following the loss of her son, Calvin. She would seclude herself in the home reading the bible, looking at pictures, and lying in Calvin's bed. She could not believe he was gone. She would constantly ask God, "Why take Calvin so soon? He is your child and he still have unfinished business in this place." Although she never got the answer, she would pray and ask for healing. She needed it because she had exhibited anger towards the man that killed her son. During the court hearing, the man who hit her son would say that "he thought he'd hit a **deer**." In an angry tone, Tonya replied, "no, you hit the thing that was most **dear** to me."

As the trial drew near, Tonya would do some self-reflection. She realized that her spiritual beliefs were not going to allow her to stay off course. She believed in healing, love, and forgiveness. The loss of Calvin not only devastated her life, but it had changed other's lives too-including the man who killed him. She knew if he had a conscious, his life could be changed forever as well. Tonya would gradually get back to doing what she and Calvin loved best-helping people. At the trial, she would stand only a few feet from the man who killed her son. She would not try to strike or fight him. She wanted justice and peace. Then she would forgive him. He'd tell her he was so sorry for what he had done. *"When you forgive, you in no way change the past-but you sure do change the future."* *(Quote by Bernard Meltzer)*.

For the next few years, Tonya continued to work with kids and help the homeless. She surrounds herself with positive friends and family. She continues her involvement in the church. To help her overcome the loneliness, she'd realize that now is a time to tell her story. She would read many books including the bible. She'd write about her life's journey and eventually put it into her first book. *(Am I your enemy because I tell you the truth by Tonya Thomas).* Today, Tonya is still writing and has also started her own publishing company.

Empty Nester

How is being an empty nester affecting your life? For most of mom's life, there were children in the house. When El passed away, she was left with sadness and had become an empty nester. She was all alone and didn't have anything to do and no one to care for. Her life has changed again. I'm sure there were periods of grief and loneliness. She didn't drive. She didn't have a significant other. She didn't go to church. Had no one to cook for but herself. Wow! This was another major change in her life. Now, for once, it's time for someone to take care of her, right.

In my opinion, we have done a great job when our kids are ready and comfortable to step out on their own. Whether it's college, military, and or straight to the job world, we love to see them become independent. That's our job as parents, right. Because of this, some of us are elated to become empty nesters. For others, they are fearing loneliness. Statistical polls show that the fear of loneliness is more prevalent with single mothers. Usually, it's because they have put a lot of things on hold to concentrate on preparing their kids for life. Now that the time has come, many single moms are uncertain on what to do next. Are you having those feelings? I have several friends who have become this way. After going through a divorce, husband dying, and gaining custody of the kids, these single moms would find resolve taking care of their kids until they were on the own. They'd hang out with girlfriends and date a little but didn't want to bring any men around their kids. Oftentimes, they would settle for a night of wining and dining. Then maybe a quick fix if you know what I mean. Sounds terrible but they didn't see any harm in it. Most of the time, it was the same guy. Hopefully, that guy would be ready to advance the relationship when the kids leave.

For one friend, that's what she thought. Her son had graduated from high school and was entering the military. She was proud of herself for helping him become a driven young man. She had lost her husband to cancer when her son was 10 years old. It would be several years later before she'd think of dating. Then she'd find a nice man on *a* dating site to hang out with from time to time. He'd tell her that he was divorced, with a couple kids-one in college and other is teenager living with his ex. He stated that he has his teenage daughter every other weekend. Nevertheless, they never spent time at each other's house. It was dinner and a movie. Then occasional hook-ups at a hotel. Her assumption was that they would spend more time together now that her son was gone but that wasn't his plan at all. See, he had gotten comfortable with the way things were and didn't want to change it. After being temporarily knocked off balance, she would distance herself from this man. Several months later, she was back on the dating site and that's how we met. Although our friendship never evolved into a relationship, we remained friends. Today, she is still single and more involved with church. She has also started a scholarship fund in honor of her late husband who was a prominent youth sports coach in the community.

Divorce, loss of loved ones, becoming an empty nester, and relocation are all events that could lead to loneliness. One of my dear friends has experience all these over the last 10 years. First, her marriage failed in 2008. Abuse, control, and infidelity had become too over-bearing. There would be periods of loneliness, but she still had 3 kids to keep her moving. The oldest son had just started college and she wanted to keep him focused. Her teenage daughter was handicap from *Rhett's Syndrome* and needs constant care. Her youngest son is a teenager too during this time and is very involved in sports and band.

In 2012, her youngest son would leave the house to start college. Everything seems to be going well. She is spending time with friends, going to church regularly, and praying every night. Well, one year later, her daughter would lose her battle with Rhett's at the age of 23. Although she was devastated with the death, she knew that the time would eventually come. See, when her daughter was diagnosed with the condition at age 5, the doctors told her that she'd be lucky to make it to teenage years. Nevertheless, not only is her entire home empty, there's emptiness inside of her life. Her marriage failed, boys are in college or starting their lives-good thing, and daughter has passed away. *Can you say knocked off balance!*

As time would pass, the youngest son would drop out of school to be there for his mom as she goes through difficult times. She would surround herself with positive friends and talk to her family members daily. She'd increase her time in church and create her personal war room wall. Prayer for strength and guidance would occur each night. To prevent loneliness from taking over, she begins to put a lot of time into work. Her project manager's job has her traveling to different states and she is contemplating on a change in her life. *(Relocation).*

In the winter of 2016, she decides to leave NC and take a job with a company in Memphis, Tn. Prior to accepting this position, she had been working there as a project manager with her company for a year. She likes the environment and the cost of living. Plus, her salary was increasing by 40%. She has created a good relationship with the upper management team and they are looking to further advance her. Within six months, the company is already sending her to their headquarters in Ireland for some training and best practices. Wow! Things are going well, right.

What she didn't expect was how lazy some of her direct reports and other teammates were. She is enduring a lot of stress due to her team's attitudes, behaviors, and performances. On top of that, she only has a couple of friends in the area to confide in. She has found a regular church and she likes it but not ready to be involved in any ministries. Meeting a prospective companion is much harder than she'd ever imagine. Her *quality of life is off-balance.* She is too consumed with work.

Furthermore, she has no one to come home to or spend time with. She is *lonely* once again. *"Funny how your quality of life improves dramatically when you surround yourself with good, intelligent, kind-hearted, positive, and loving people."* (MoveMe Quotes). Although she has these kind of friends, they're not near. She's praying that God will surround her with these type friends where she currently resides. She realizes that this is not how she wants to spend her life. She didn't envision the relocation, greater opportunity, and money would come in an exchange for her quality of life. Because she is a woman of God, she believes that he has her there for a purpose.

Also, that he will give her guidance and direction. Today, she remains upbeat. She has put her trust and faith in God. She has started to be a little more involved in the church. She helps the needy in the church. She takes time-out for family, especially her grandson. She has also started writing her own book which will depict women's roles in leadership but not just the business aspects. Can't wait to read it!

Does loneliness have you out of balance today? Do you fear loneliness? Have you or are you living your life vicariously through your kids or someone else? What will you do when they are gone? We are not with each other on the earth forever but God is always with us. *"Behold, the hour is coming, indeed it has come, when you will be scattered, each to his own home, and will leave me alone. Yet I am not alone, for the Father is with me." (John 16:32).* If we trust and believe in God, we will be ready when the time comes. We all should stay humble for the times we have shared with each other.

You would imagine that no one wants to be alone; yet, many people are content with their situation. At least, that's what we say. The discontentment felt from past relationships has left many people feeling lonely. Some loneliness comes from circumstances that are out of your control; such as being left alone in my mom's situation. It's understandable that sadness comes when you lose your companion for life and loneliness takes place. The fond memories are some of the things that help loved ones get past it. In many instances such as divorce, death, and empty nester, it is scary when you realize that the person that you have cared for or whom cared for you is gone. Most situations are a part of life and you must trust and believe that you can pull yourself together. *"It is the Lord who goes before you. He will be with you; he will not leave or forsake you. Do not fear of be dismayed." (Deuteronomy 31:8).*

Chapter 8

Sexual Abuse

Sexual abuse is any sort of non-consensual sexual contact. Sexual abuse can happen to men and women of any age. Sexual abuse by a partner or intimate companion can include derogatory name calling, refusal to use contraception, deliberately causing unwanted physical pain during sex. It also includes deliberately passing on sexual diseases or infections to someone. The use of objects, toys, and other items (baby oil or lubricants) without consent and to cause pain and humiliation are also examples of sexual abuse. (pandys.org). Think about these sentences for a moment. Has any of this happened to you? Do you know someone who has encountered this type of sexual abuse? Has it **knocked you or someone you know off balance?** How has it affected your life or someone else's life that you know?

As you see, there are many forms of sexual abuse. Any of these events could change a victim's course of life. Oftentimes, the victims become abusers themselves. The **Me-Too movement** going on in our entertainment industry has brought to light a lot of sexual assaults from the past. Victims have gotten the courage to speak up about those incidents. I'm not sure if it's going to give them peace or help them find resolve but at least they know that they're not alone. For many of these victims who were trying to get a break into entertainment, it came with a price. Fearing the loss of opportunities or that big break, many of them complied with the circumstances. Although the encounters were humiliating, many of them got their break. Of course, they also had a choice. Can you imagine the number of victims who were lied to and didn't get that break!

Think about those victims of sexual abuse who didn't have a choice! The ones who were held at gunpoint, by knife, threatened to be killed if they screamed, or left in the middle of nowhere. How about the young boys who were promised a good life, then sexually abused by Jerry Sandusky! How about young girls and boys who have been kidnapped and become sex slaves! All these victims were left with physical and mental scars. Fearing judgement, many were reluctant to come forward. The **Me-Too movement** is helping many gain that courage. *"Be strong and courageous. Do not fear or be in dread of them, for it is the Lord your God who goes with you. He will not leave or forsake you." (Deuteronomy 31:6).*

On the other hand, this movement has **knocked the perpetrators and their families off balance too**. It has shocked idolizers, friends, and audiences. Embarrassment/shame, humiliation, loss of friends, loss of endorsements, and or careers are all threatened. We hope that all these families are grounded. If God has not been incorporated in their lives, now is the time. Hopefully, some of their past transgressions from the previous life were mentioned prior to their marriage and or start of a family.

As far as we know, Mr. Scott was not a victim of sexual abuse. His womanizing ways may have led to some sexual abuse, but we wouldn't know about it. Towards the end of the marriage with mom, he would call her derogatory names in front of some of the kids such as slut and fat ass. Of course, he wasn't man enough to say it to her face. It never dawned on him that he was the reason for her transgressions and or transformations. When he left her and the kids, they all were unprotected. We don't know if our brother, Randy, would have been raped or not had Mr. Scott been in the home. We do know that the possibility would not have been as great because Randy probably wouldn't have been out so late. Nevertheless, it happened, and Mr. Scott was not around nor did he come to support his son during the ordeal. His thoughts would probably be on the same lines as those when his older son was slapped by the farm supervisor. *"Randy should have had his ass home before dark,"* would have been his response. I wonder what percentage of sexual abuse victims are the result of being unprotected by loved ones because they didn't think anything would happen or they were too caught up being selfish and thoughtless.

Randy was physically and emotionally knocked off balance. Before his own personal lifestyle could begin, it is altered. His potential angel-like wings hadn't formed before having his innocence taken away by a man from *Sodom* (*Genesis 19:1-38*). This unexpected event would scar our brother for the remainder of his life. Although mom would pray and do all she could to comfort Randy through his healing process, the trauma would affect him through the remainder of his childhood. He was needing counseling and guidance from someone other than mom. She just had too many other responsibilities and no financial resources to seek help. Over the next few years, Randy would drop out of school and distant himself from friends and family. He would start working in the local tobacco fields. He would use a lot of his money to buy cigarettes and beer. He would become belligerent and disobedient to everyone. The attention he was needing, mom or no one else in the house could give to him. She would offer church counseling to him but couldn't force him to go. Plus, he would state that, 'the church is full of *faggets*."

When Randy turned 16, he left the house. His first journey was to High Point where two sisters, another brother, and cousins were living. Both sisters were married, and the brother was living with a girlfriend. The oldest sister and her husband were the only ones who had room for him to stay, which was on the couch. They had two kids, a son who was two years old and a daughter who was five. He would seek work, but wasn't having much success. There weren't many tobacco fields in this area and local jobs for teenagers under 18 required you to be in school. He would wander the streets looking for work. From time to time, he would be asked to babysit while our sister ran errands and the husband was at work.

While his little nephew was sleeping, he would play with his niece. Initially, it was just innocent play, but my brother had a motive. He didn't take this kind of time to play with his own little sisters and brothers. Nevertheless, he would start touching her inappropriately. He would have her sit in his lap and play bouncy, bouncy. The fun and laughter she was having would turn into pain and confusion. The *molestation* has occurred, and he has warned her not to say a word or he would harm her more. A lot of crying would occur prior to her mom leaving for errands again and our sister just brushed it off as though her daughter was being a baby, not realizing what was happening. Randy would have this *devilish* grin on his face. Ironically, his younger siblings and nephews would talk about that grin of his when he would get drunk and act out. Little did we know, he had committed such acts.

The molestation would happen several times. When our niece tried to tell her parents, Randy would step into the room, scare her, and she would go numb. Randy had become a pedophile. He is acting *"without natural affection"*. *(Romans 1:31)*. Although in the bible, this type of behavior is an **Abomination** and death is pursuant. But, God forgives all who repent for their sins. Plus, he rose Jesus from death to forgive all our sins. Randy didn't feel his actions were sinful and he had no trust in God and repentance is out of the question. Therefore, he is still susceptible to molesting others. *(resurrection.wordpress.com)*.

Randy would become a wanderer. He would spend time in Charleston, SC with an aunt and cousins, Florida with cousins, and Rochester, NY with uncles over the next 10 years. While in Rochester, he was living with one of our uncles who had seven kids in the house (3 boys and 4 girls). Randy was around 18 yrs. old and a couple of uncle's kids were around the same age. The girls were 2 to a room with the youngest ones at age ten and eight in the same room. Randy slept on the couch in the family room. One night following some heavy drinking, Randy would creep into the bedroom of the youngest two girls and molest them both. *"But he would not listen to her, and being stronger than she, he violated her and lay with her." (2*

Samuel 13:14). Wow! How bold and corrupted he must have been! Apparently, he did not fear any consequences following his behaviors.

Randy's mind seemed to have been infiltrated by Satan. He needed help but he had to first realize that he has a problem. I wonder what would have happened if my uncle would have turned Randy into authorities. One would hope for counseling and rehabilitation, but it could have been the total opposite. Nevertheless, Randy was punishing others because of what happened to him. Maybe he didn't feel as though he could live a normal life. *"Don't judge yourself by what others have done to you." (Quote by C. Kennedy, goodreads.com).*

While Randy was out with the boys the next day, the two girls would inform their mother of the encounter. Irate, the mother would summon her husband and tell him what happened and to get Randy out as soon as possible or she would hurt him. Nevertheless, Randy would be kicked out with no repercussions. Another uncle would allow him to stay until he made enough money to leave Rochester. The two cousins would grow up to be beautiful, normal, young ladies. They would have nightmares and fears, but their strength and courage would keep them moving forward.

Randy would continue wandering for the next fifteen to twenty years, up and down the east coast. It's unknown how many other family members or young lady's lives if any he had **knocked off balance** on his journey. He never got married or had kids of his own that we know of. His life would be full of **alcohol abuse** until he was terminally ill. He didn't even have a steady girlfriend until his late 40's. The blow that he endured as a child would linger on for the rest of his life. Randy would succumb to *cancer* in May of 2007. The knowledge of the molestations didn't surface among the family until after Randy's death. According to my cousins, my mom knew about Randy molesting them because her brother let her know. I don't think she knew about the grandchild, but she seemed to have some inclination when the niece came to live with us.

We had another niece who was sexually abused. She was a senior in high school. We knew who her boyfriend was but unaware of the event until years later. We often wondered why she was dating him anyway. She was a pretty, smart young lady. While he was a drop-out and a bum. He drank a lot and didn't have much going for himself. Apparently, she had some *low self-esteem*. Nevertheless, she took the school bus to his house one afternoon. He was the only one home at the time. He knew that his little brothers and sister would be home within the next hour. He had been drinking and assumed his girlfriend came over for sex. After dating for a couple months, this was the first time being completely alone. Sex was not her intentions that day. She just wanted to spend time with him. Unfortunately, he was determined to have sex and he subdued and *raped* her that day. **Can you say knocked off balance!** She couldn't believe what had happened. His little siblings and his mom would arrive moments after the encounter.

In shock and pain, she didn't know what to do. She didn't want to call her mom because she shouldn't be at her boyfriend's house anyway. She would get herself together and ask his mom to take her home. She'd go into the house, take a shower, and to go bed early. Hours later, her mom would come home and see her lying down in the bed. Our niece would not disclose to her mom what happened. Two months later and no menstrual cycle. She is pregnant at 18 and still in high school. Wow! Ashamed and embarrassed, she'd tell her mom what happened and that she's pregnant. She'd tell her mom that she's not ready to be a mother and ask to be taken to the clinic for an *abortion*.

Although God doesn't condone abortions in the bible, it doesn't state what should happen from a pregnancy of rape. *"I form the light, and create darkness: I make peace, and create evil: I the LORD do all these things." (Isaiah 45:7, KJV)*. Our niece would ask her mom not to tell anyone. It was embarrassing enough to say she was raped and not seek justice or medical assistance. Plus, it's shameful enough that she's had an abortion and she doesn't want to feel ostracized by the family for what she has done. It doesn't help them when their parents or guardians try to keep the events silent and act as though nothing happened.

Secrecy by victims is like *denial*. No one knows what victims are going through without knowing what is bothering them. The fear of people being judgmental overcomes the victims. Victims often feel ashamed. Little do they realize that many others have been through the same circumstance. Talking about it or talking through it is the beginning of healing.

According to Darkness of Light, a Charleston-based sex abuse organization, one in seven girls and one in twenty-five boys will be sexually abused by the age of eighteen.

Statistics on Perpetrators of Child Sex Abuse(victimsofcrime.org)

- *Offenders are overwhelmingly male, ranging from adolescents to the elderly (page 171).*
- *Some perpetrators are female. It is estimated that women are the abusers in about 14% of cases reported among boys and 6% of cases reported among girls.*
- *Approximately one-third of offenders are themselves juveniles (page 172).*
- *23% of reported cases of child sexual abuse are perpetrated by individuals under the age of 18 (page 3)*
- *Only 14% of children who suffered sexual abuse were violated by an unknown perpetrator (page 172).*
- *60% of children are sexually abused by someone in their social circle. Hence, the phrase "Stranger Danger" is misleading (page 172).*

- *Meta-analysis estimates that 14% of sexual offenders commit another sexual offense after five years, 24% after fifteen years (page 172).*
- *Child Maltreatment 2010 reports that 6.2% of child abusers sexually abused a child (page 77).*
- *40-80% of juvenile sex offenders have themselves been victims of sexual abuse (Advances in Clinical Child Psychology, page 19).*

The effects from sexual abuse are very devastating. The blow from the event could **change or determine one's course of life**. Many victims put themselves in seclusion. Many grow up to be predators or pedophiles. Some become introverts or can't cope with the normal world. A lot of victims fear any type of sexual relationship with the opposite sex. While others crave sex regularly. Nevertheless, there's a misconception that all victims fall into these categories but a large portion of them go on to live normal lives. The possibility of becoming sex abusers is more prevalent in poor and or dysfunctional families. How are you coping as a sexual abused victim? Do you fall into one of these categories? Have you reported your abuse? Too many cases go unreported due to fear, shame/embarrassment, shock, not wanting to feel ostracized, or story is unbelievable. When you don't report the abuse, the perpetrator gets a free pass to find another victim. So long as it's not you. right? Do you care?

Although my niece wouldn't tell of her abuse until she was

an adult or seek any counseling for it, she would go on to live a normal life. She would marry a minister and have two beautiful kids. Later, she would go back to college earning a degree in counseling. How ironic! Today, she is a licensed professional counselor in mental health for people ten years and older. She specializes in helping clients with a vast array of issues related to mental health including sex abuse.

My two cousins grew up to live normal lives as well. They both attended many church retreats and camps that instilled the importance of family, trust, guidance, protection, and service to God. They both received college educations. They got married and have kids and grandkids. Currently, one has recently moved back to Rochester with her husband, kids, and grandkids. She is working in insurance as a manager of workers compensation and risk management. She volunteers in the community to help at risk kids and feeding the homeless. The other cousin received a degree in information systems and worked as an IT specialist for many years. She had to stop working due to hereditary kidney disease. She has spoken at many seminars in NY and NC on sexual education, diabetes, and kidney disease. Although the molestation knocked each of them off-balance, the blows did not determine their course of life. They are all living proof that through love, support, and the guidance of the Lord, everything can work out just fine.

For those of us who have never been a victim of sexual abuse, it's hard to relate with those who have. I would imagine that all situations are different. Being groped and or using sexual gestures and words are surely different than being raped or molested! Oftentimes, you're able to stop a person from groping you or making you feel uncomfortable. You can turn them in to your boss or police. Never should we allow sexual assaults to happen if we have a choice! I know it's easier said than done.

Nevertheless, recovering from sexual assaults whether physically or mentally takes time. Blaming yourself for what someone did to you is not the way to start coping! Also, taking your frustration out on others or becoming an abuser, is not the way to go either. In due time, the perpetrators will have their day with the Lord. *"Beloved, never avenge yourselves, but leave it to the wrath of God, for it is written, "Vengeance is mine, I will repay, says the Lord." (Romans 12:19)*. Overcoming the fear, gaining strength, and courage may require some help. It's okay to talk with counselors, loved ones, and or God. Your personal healing may entail telling your story to others in hope that it prevents sexual assaults from happening to them.

Chapter 9

Alcohol and Drug Abuse

Why do people abuse drugs and alcohol?

Here are some of the Top 10 reasons that people become drug and alcohol abusers according to *recoveryconnection.com*.

- *Some drugs are legal*
  Alcohol and nicotine are not only both legal drugs, but they are the most <u>commonly abused drugs</u>.
- *They get a Prescription for drugs*
  There is a huge misconception that just because a doctor prescribed drugs they are safe. Prescription drugs are every bit as dangerous and addictive as street drugs like <u>cocaine</u> and <u>heroin</u>.
- *Going against the grain*
  Young adults and teenagers often start to abuse drugs because they are not sure where they fit in. Rebelling by abusing drugs and alcohol is not uncommon among young adults. What can start off as "fun" and "recreational" can quickly turn into an uncontrollable addiction.

- *Feelings of emptiness*
  Addiction often starts when an individual feel lonely. They turn to drugs and alcohol thinking that it will fill a void that they have been living with.

- *Peer Pressure*
  Teenagers and adults can succumb to peer pressure. The pressure of being around others who are abusing

drugs or alcohol can make anyone follow suit and do things that they never thought they would.

- *Drugs and alcohol can make you feel good*
  People commonly fall into addiction because they begin using drugs to mask emotions that they are going through. The abuse makes them feel good and forget about the problem at hand. Eventually they think they can't live without drugs.

- *Drugs and alcohol are more available than ever*
  Prescription drugs, street drugs and alcohol are more available than ever. Prescription drugs can be obtained on the streets, through doctors and even online. Where there is a will there is a way.

- *Alcohol isn't enough*
  Oftentimes, addiction starts with alcohol but when the effects of alcohol are not what they used to be the addict turns to harder and stronger drugs.

- *Experimenting*
  It is not uncommon for addiction to stem from a person being curious and experimenting with drugs. It is a scenario that often starts with alcohol or marijuana but ends up with cocaine, prescription medication or even crystal meth and heroin.

- *Self-Medicating*
  People from all different backgrounds use alcohol to unwind at the end of the day or prescription drugs to help them cope with stress of everyday life. Patterns like this can quickly turn into addiction.

Can you relate to any of these circumstances?

As we look back on mom's life, there are many other reasons that people might abuse drugs and alcohol. There were a series of events that **knocked her and her loved ones off balance (Death, Abandonment, Infidelity, Rape, Ostracized, Gun Violence, Loneliness, Poverty, etc.).** Of course, this list can go on and on. Although these things may be past events, they are all present in many of our lives today. Furthermore, they all could possibly lead to drug and alcohol abuse. Think about the blows that you've been hit with! Have they led you to abusing alcohol and drugs? How is the abuse affecting your life? Are you a functional or dysfunctional abuser? Or, are you in denial and don't believe you are an abuser at all?

Alcohol Abuse

Mr. Scott abused alcohol during the marriage. Initially, he drank socially because he felt it was normal, the way he was wired in his lifestyle. Later, the drinking increased to almost daily. The reasons for his increased drinking was unknown but it appeared to be *stress and anxiety*. Most of this was self-induced. Mr. Scott was uncertain about his marriage. He did not envision a long future. He married mom for the wrong reasons and he had no faith in God. For if he did, this would have been God's message to him. *"For I know the plans I have for you, declares the Lord, plans for welfare and not for evil, to give you a future and a hope." (Jeremiah 29:11).* Now, he has a bunch of kids to take care of and this was not his plan. Furthermore, he doesn't really want to work for an honest living. Therefore, he used alcohol as his escape from being a father, provider, husband, and communicator. In fact, it was his way of *avoiding* communication completely.

Some of the older siblings would emulate their dad's pattern of drinking. If you can recall from an earlier chapter, the oldest son passed away at the age of 56 from *Cirrhosis*. Prior to his illness, he was drinking approximately a half pint of vodka daily. He was a functional drinker and we're not sure if there was an underlying reason for his abuse. He wasn't married and didn't have any kids as well. He worked a steady job. Maybe he just wasn't so happy with his life and drinking helped him cope.

Our brother, Randy, was a chronic alcohol abuser as an adult too. His drink of choice was **MD20-20** and **Wild Irish Rose** wine. It was the cheap wine with the high potency. He consumed approximately a pint per day for over a decade. His abuse was related to the inability to cope from being raped as a child. Of course, the alcohol abuse would contribute to *stomach cancer* which led to his death. A couple of our sisters would abuse alcohol heavily as well. Their reasons were related to past events and the way their lives had turned out. The abuse would lead to other health issues. Doctors would warn them to stop drinking or it would kill them. They would recommend **Alcohol Treatment Centers,** but my sisters didn't want to go. Either they didn't believe anything would happen to them or they just refused to let go. Or, maybe they had forsaken God and the devil was in their ear. They did not have the will power to quit. Mom could not persuade them to because she couldn't relate. See, mom was not an alcohol abuser. In fact, I never seen her drink any type of alcohol. She had enough things occurring in her life without the enticement of alcohol or anything else. Nevertheless, Alcohol Anonymous says that oftentimes it takes a recovering alcoholic to help an alcoholic. Eventually, they would succumb too soon due to complications related to alcohol abuse. Are you allowing alcohol abuse to affect your health? Have you considered reaching out for help with the abuse? Are you ignoring all the warning signs? Don't wait too long and allow the effects to hit you with multiple blows!

One of my good friends and work colleague had a near death experience from the abuse of alcohol. He was a star defensive tackle in college. His ability would lead him to a short stint in the NFL. Upon completing his football career, he'd hang out with old college buddies **partying** and drinking. Before he knew it, he had become an alcohol abuser. Like my oldest brother, he was a functional drinker. He'd work a normal 7-4 M-F job and help coach junior football during the week. Football was his passion and he was ecstatic to be out on the field coaching little kids-giving them his knowledge of the game. When Friday evenings rolled around, the work week is over and time to *"Turn Up."* Tired from the week and hung over from drinking on Friday, he would often miss the kids early Saturday morning football games. Those kids were looking for his guidance and he was home recovering. Why get their hopes up high and not be there to help them follow through!

One Friday night after drinking heavily with friends, he was driving home drunk, and nodded off on the interstate, losing control of his Bronco, and driving under a tractor trailer semi-truck. The impact would take the top of his vehicle off, nearly taking his head off. **Can you say knocked off balance!** Unable to open the driver's side door due to it being pinned shut, he'd climb over the back seat and out of the back door. As he climbed out, his knee would land on a bible in his backseat. Wow! He would look and see what it was and grab it. He hadn't seen that bible in nearly 8 years; plus, he had forgotten it was even there. He'd say that, *"God was with me during that crash. He was not ready to let me go. There was too much unfinished business in store for me."*

"Be alert and of sober mind. Your enemy the devil prowls around like a roaring lion looking for someone to devour. Resist him, standing firm in the faith, because you know that the family of believers throughout the world is undergoing the same kind of sufferings. And the God of all

*grace, who called you to his eternal glory in Christ, after you
have suffered a little while, will himself restore you and make
you strong, firm and steadfast." (1 Peter 5:8-10).*

This would be his wake-up call and **change his course of
life**. Upon recovery from his minor injuries, he would check into
Alcohol Anonymous classes. He would attend every day for 90
consecutive days-even through the Thanksgiving and Christmas
holidays. He would continue the AA classes but not on a
regular basis. You see, once you've entered into the program,
it's a lifetime engagement. It gives the recovering alcoholics a
chance to possibly save someone's life with their story. He'd
have an occasional relapse, but it would only last for a couple
drinks. Eventually, he would quit completely. He'd still hang
out from time to time with the fellows but try to encourage
them to stop drinking. He'd get back into going to church
regularly. He'd start coaching junior pro football again-this time
making all the games.

A couple years later, he'd meet his princess and get
married. She would encourage him to become more involved
with **church** and to become a mentor to young teenage males,
especially at-risk ones. He would instruct them on the
importance of living well and doing the right thing. He'd also
teach them basic manners and how to treat people and earn
the same respect. He'd also teach them basic work ethics such

as: cutting grass, cleaning the house, changing oil and tires on cars, earning a check, balancing a checking account, etc. Most importantly, he'd teach them that it's ok to "say no to the temptations in life." God will be proud of you. *"For I say, walk by the Spirit, and you will not carry out the desire of the flesh." (Galatians 5:16).*

Today, he has been sober for over sixteen years. He is a Deacon in his church and presides over one of the men's ministries. He continues to mentor young men. He works continuously on improving his relationship with Jesus Christ. He and his wife have a beautiful daughter for whom they cherish and teach the importance of knowing Jesus. He has gotten a promotion on his job and went back to school and obtained his Master's Degree. Well done my friend!

Have you had one of these near-death experiences? What happened? Did it knock you off balance and change your course of life? How? What positive changes have you made since the event? Have you incorporated Jesus or a higher power?

Drug Abuse

The crack cocaine epidemic hit the US by storm in the late 80's. The effects ripped through many communities especially urban communities. The inexpensive drug was giving vulnerable people a quick high and a euphoric feeling. It was the release that many people felt they needed. Unfortunately, many became addicted to the drug. Initially, that $10, 10-minute high was nothing. Then, the 10 minutes wasn't enough. People were wanting the high to last most of the day. Before they realized it, some were spending $100-500 a day.

It was an easy drug for pushers and drug dealers to sell. It was in small, rock forms which made it a quick pass and go for some. Money for the dealers and pushers was so easily made that many were not looking for other occupations. People were enjoying the high so much that they were depleting bank accounts, retirement funds, losing their homes and jobs all for that high. When all resources were lost, they would result to anything to get that fix (stealing, robbing, prostitution, etc.). Many abusers had **knocked** themselves and their loved one's lives completely *off balance*. The effects would change or determine their course of life. Many families would be broken, lives were lost due to overdose, disease and other health issues would form, and murders would occur.

Were you a drug abuser? Are you still abusing drugs? What toll has it taken on your life? How have you winged yourself off the substance? Do you have people in your current circle with a drug problem? Can you see it potentially knocking them or their loved one's off balance? Are you offering any help or guidance for them? Do you pray for yourself or your loved ones who are drug abusers?

In the early to mid-90's, there were several siblings hooked on crack cocaine. Their reasons were **peer pressure, stress from job, undiagnosed depression, fear of failure, and past hang-ups.** The effects caused a lot of turmoil in their family circles. That moment of needing that fix to get through the day turned out to be daily. The encouragement and advice that family members were offering was looked upon as talking down to them. They had become selfish and didn't care. *"Do nothing from selfishness or empty conceit, but with humility of mind, regard one another as more important than yourselves, do not merely look out for your own personal interests, but also for the interests of others." (Philippians 2:3-4).* The thought of God and or prayer was the furthest thing from their minds.

Two of the siblings were married and not only were they addicted to the drugs, but their spouses were as well. One lived in New Jersey while the other lived in mom's neighborhood. Another brother, who lived in New Jersey as well, didn't have kids nor a girlfriend and he felt that he had nothing to lose. Our sister, who lived locally and a single mom with four kids, was leaving them **unprotected** when she was on her binges. Although a couple of her kids were teenagers, they had the freedom to do whatever because it appeared there would be no consequences. Luckily, the teenage daughter had good morals and would look after the younger two. On the other hand, the older teenage son would start hanging out with the wrong crowd which would temporarily shape his life.

Mom would worry constantly about all of them. What some of the movies and news were depicting of drug fiends is what she was seeing from her kids. The two local siblings were out in the streets all night long looking for a fix. They'd often come by mom's house asking for money. They are hyper and fidgety at times, she said. Although they may have come across as scary, mom didn't have any fear except for their own well-being. She would have long prayers for them.

Oftentimes when I came home to visit, I would get a chance to see all the local siblings and we'd gather at mom's house. Later, we would meet at one of the older sister's house to socialize, eat, drink, and play cards. It was always a good, traditional thing to do. Nevertheless, I wouldn't see the two with the substance problem for long. Maybe, it was because they knew how I felt about the unnecessary anxiety they were placing on mom. Nevertheless, as soon as I'd leave to go back to Tennessee, they go by mom's asking for money again. See, they knew that I'd always leave her some money to buy herself some things. **Wow!**

Here are some statistics on crack cocaine from treatment-centers.net**:**

- One out of four people have used cocaine in some form at least once in their lives.
- 3.3 percent of students who are in college and high school in the U.S. either have tried crack cocaine once, or are active users of the drug.
- The U.S Drug Enforcement Administration made 3,921 arrests for crack cocaine during Fiscal Year 2004.
- The Substance Abuse and Mental Health Services Administration reports that in 2007 there were 167,914 admissions to treatment centers due to crack cocaine addiction, and the average age of those admitted was 39.
- According to the 2008 National Survey on Drug Use and Health, 8.4 million Americans aged 12 or older reported trying crack cocaine at least once during their lifetimes – that's 3.4% of the population aged 12 or older.
- The same survey revealed that 150,000 young people ages 12 to 17, and more than one million people ages 18 to 25 have used crack cocaine at least once.

Crack cocaine is still a highly used drug. Today, it is overshadowed by the **Opioid Epidemic** which unlike crack, it is affecting more than the urban communities. Ironically, our government is creating a lot of assistance programs for people with opioids addiction. We didn't see much government intervention for the crack cocaine epidemic. **Hmmm.....**

Nevertheless, are you or your loved ones a victim of these epidemics? Is help being sought? How about prayer and guidance from God?

One of the brothers would have a positive ending to years of drug abuse. He is the fifteenth child and nearly my twin even though we are a year and a half apart in age. The older we've gotten, the more we look alike. We were inseparable as kids-hanging out in the neighborhood, at the pool hall, and playing sports. Once we became teenagers, puberty and friends would change that. See, peer pressure and the desire for constant fun would lead him to quit sports and hang out at nightclubs with his friends. He was a little more girl crazy than I was. Furthermore, he would experiment with marijuana early in life. As years passed, he would enter community college and pick back up on sports. He would meet some new friends and start to experiment with marijuana laced with cocaine. He enjoyed the high but wasn't hooked. He'd continue his education, transfer to a liberal arts college, be a member of the men's basketball and baseball teams, and earn a bachelor of science degree. All the while, he would still crave that high and seek that fix. He was a functional drug abuser. Not only was he a user, he sold drugs in college to get extra money. Can you relate?

After graduating from college, he moved back home. He would get married and rent his first house. He would have a hard time finding a job in his field of study because he had a felony charge at the age of 18 for forging a check. Although the fines were paid, and the charges dismissed, it still showed on his record. So, he would work as a substitute teacher and become the basketball coach for the local middle school. His wife would get a job with **Pinehurst Golf Club**-a prestigious professional golf resort in the area. Things are going ok. He is earning respect from the school administration and the boys' basketball team is doing well. But, there is some frustration because he knows he could be a full-time teacher with better pay if only the forgery charge was expunged.

Before you knew it, he was buying rocks of cocaine. He and his wife would smoke them together. The high had them wanting more and more. Suddenly, they are selling and pawning items from their home to get money for the fix. His wife would be caught stealing at the country club and get fired. He would continue working as a substitute teacher but quit after one of his students seen him going into a crack house. He didn't want that to get around in the school and further destroy his image. By now, mom is aware of what's going on and she is worried senseless. He is coming by her home asking for money. She would ask, "what is going on with you." He'd reply, "I'm a little down right now and I have some things going on but working on them." Mom knew better than that. She'd encourage him to get his self together before something terrible happens. She'd tell him to pray and she'd pray for him too. *"Cast your burden on the Lord, and he shall sustain you; he shall never permit the righteous to be moved." (*<u>Psalm 55:22</u>*).*

He would find other jobs, but quit after the first paycheck. His wife would do the same. This pattern would continue for several years. They'd get the paycheck and then blow it on crack cocaine. The addiction had become so bad that they are both in the streets trying to get a fix. They were bumming money from family and friends-not to pay bills but to get high. Now, they have exhausted all their means. You can imagine the offers they'd give the pushers. They have allowed the addiction to take over their mind, body, and spirit. *"Or do you not know that your body is a temple of the Holy Spirit within you, whom you have from God? You are not your own, for you were bought with a price. So, glorify God in your body." (*<u>Corinthians 6:19-20</u>*).*

Evicted from their home and not able to live with family, they'd move across country to California to a half-way house for addicts. They'd attend classes, find work, gradually start recovery. Six months later, they'd become impatient, home sick, and feeling out of place. They would get paid, go out on the streets of Northern California and find a fix. Not wanting the group home to become suspicious, they'd would prepare to leave when they get the next paycheck. Although not reformed, they would journey back to NC. They would go right back to the streets looking for a fix. His wife would not show up some nights and he began to fear the worst. They would agree to separate and work on their addiction independently. She would move in with her mom and her two kids.

While separated, he would journey to New Jersey where he'd be around some family in the hopes of getting his act together but that only lasted a few months. He was hanging out with another brother who was getting high as well. So, he came back home and reconnected with one of the guys who got him started with the crack. This guy was always jealous of my brother's education and communicating abilities. Nevertheless, he convinced him to go to Oklahoma to start a new life. What was he thinking! The journey didn't go well at all. They would argue and literally fight over smoking and dealing crack. *"Make no friendship with a man given to anger, nor go with a wrathful man, lest you learn his ways and entangle yourself in a snare." (Proverbs 22:24-24).* My brother gets his wake-up call and realizes that he must **change his current friends and his environment**.

It is now the fall of 2003. My brother and his wife had been on this binge for nearly 10 years. He checks himself into a drug treatment center in northeastern NC for 2 weeks then into a halfway house for 2 more weeks. He is thankful that he has his sanity, health, and disease free. He begins to pray and read his bible each night-recalling mom's words to him. During his time in the halfway house, he has made connections with people on potential jobs in his field-Social Work. He'd also meet an attorney who said he would help him get his forgery expunged. **Isn't God good when you're walking with him?** After leaving the halfway house, he would go home and give mom a big hug and tell her thank you. He would promise to her and himself that the previous life is over. *"You were taught, with regards to your former way of life, to put off your old self, which is being corrupted by its deceitful desires; to be made new in the attitude of your minds; and to put on the new self, created to be like God in true righteousness and holiness."* *(Ephesians 4:22-24)*. Unfortunately, he and his wife would remain separated and eventually divorce.

Within a year, he would land a job in Social Work. He'd save up enough money to buy his own house. He'd become involved with children's outreach programs in the area. He would participate in counseling services at the Juvenile Delinquent center at Morrison Training camp. He would get involved with youth sports which includes refereeing and umpiring basketball, football, and baseball. He and his wife would divorce, and he would remarry a few years later. He now has a son whom he adores and is working extremely hard on being a good father. He has been drug-free for 14 years. Although he doesn't attend church on a regular basis, he reads his bible every night and thanks God for all he has done for him. *"Be joyful always; pray continually; give thanks in all circumstances, for this is God's will for you in Christ Jesus." (Thessalonians 5:16-18).*

Why do many of us abuse drugs and alcohol? Oftentimes, many people drink and use drugs to celebrate milestones and accomplishments. Sometimes, the abuse comes while just hanging out with friends. Others abuse these substances to help them cope with life, disappointments, pain, stress, loss of loved ones, anxiety/stress, etc. Little do we realize that it's only a temporary fix. We know there are potential consequences to the abuse but many of us don't have any fear. Family and friends try to encourage you to seek help, but you don't think there's a problem. Before you know it, you are addicted and began to lose everything. The selfishness has knocked a lot of lives off balance. *"The end of all things is at hand; therefore, be self-controlled and sober-minded for the sake of your prayers. (1 Peter 4:7).* What good has come from your substance abuse? Intervention, counseling, and prayer may become necessary before things get worse.

Chapter 10

Gun Violence (Senseless Acts)

If you watch the news, reading posts on social media, or reading the newspapers, you're hearing of senseless deaths by gun violence every day. There are terrorist attacks all over the world, police brutality has risen, mentally disturbed people with guns, and gang related deaths by gun continues to plague our nation. Terrorist attacks with guns in the U.S has resulted in many deaths over the past 15 years. 13 people were gunned down in Fort Hood, Texas in 2009, 14 in San Bernardino, Ca. in 2015, 49 killed in a nightclub shooting in Orlando, Fla. in 2016, 9 killed in a church in Charleston, SC and many more in the US. _(fivethirtyeight.com)._ Of course, who can forget the children and teachers killed in Sandy Hook, Conn in 2012., or the sniper attacks in the Washington DC/Virginia area in 2002. Recently, the mass shooting in Las Vegas has changed many lives and puts us all on alert. All these events were senseless acts that **knocked loved ones off balance**. Many lives will never be the same. The sad thing is that these acts will continue to happen until we, as a country, can come up with some better control.

In 2016, there were 963 people killed by police in the US. Forty-eight of them were unarmed and 39 of the 48 were black. Body cameras were in place on 139 of those events. It was discovered later that 231 of the victims had some form of mental illness. According to the *chicagotribune.com*, the city of Chicago alone recorded 762 murders due to gun violence in 2016. Although most of those deaths were gang related, they all were senseless. What are the driving forces to so much gun violence in our world? Is it **fear, religion, racism/hatred, training or lack thereof, poverty, drugs, territory, money or lack thereof, power, gang initiation, mental illness, etc.?**

Are there family members or someone in your circle who has been killed or killed someone with a gun? Were they in the military at war (**Armed Forces**)? Were they protecting and serving our communities (**Police Officer**)? Were they protecting their homes and or family from unlawful property entry or trespassing? Have you ever shot and killed someone because they were trying to kill you or someone in your circle? (**Self-defense**). Wow! All these questions would have answers that are justifiable, right. Is this what we think of when we are exercising our **2nd Amendment rights**? The world we live in today is totally transformed from the biblical days. Swords, spheres, and rocks are rarely heard of as weapons used for protection and hunting. Nevertheless, the bible's reference of how or what weapons should be used for should still exist, right. Unless corruption has invaded (Satan), and the weapons are used to strike fear, to commit robbery, and murder. *"When a strong man, fully armed, guards his own palace, his goods are safe; but when one stronger than he attacks him and overcomes him, he takes away his armor in which he trusted and divides his spoil." (Luke 11:21-22).*

During a conversation on guns long ago, mom told me that her dad owned a shotgun when she was a -little girl. He used it to hunt deer, squirrels, and rabbits. She said he'd offer to teach each of them how to shoot it. She stated that she was too afraid, but several other brothers and sisters learned how to use it. He kept it hidden from all so they wouldn't try to get it while he was away. He would reference protecting the home from intruders but never once saying I'll kill someone. I believe my grandfather was familiar with *Luke 11.* She'd also say that her husband carried a pistol. She wasn't sure if it was to protect his home and family or to protect himself from his wrong doings outside of the home. Her boyfriend also owned a shotgun for which he was using it to hunt as well. He kept it in her bedroom, but it was in site. Oftentimes, we (younger boys) contemplated on testing it out. I can imagine mom's reaction.

That cold winter day in 1970, my oldest sister's husband was shot and killed at a party while she sat beside him. Prior to the shooting, he was questioning this man about flirting with his wife. The man got defensive as though he was being threatened. He went outside to his car and came back in with a pistol. He pointed the gun at my brother- in- law and asked him, *"who's the bad ass now mother-fucker."* Fearless, brother-in-law told my sister don't worry as she was screaming. He put his head back on the couch and said, *"so, you're gonna shoot me over some dumb shit."* The man fired one shot striking my brother-in-law in the neck and killing him. **Can you say knocked off balance!**

Not only was this a **senseless act**, but a person is killed. The victim's loved one's course of life has changed completely. The shooter's course of life has changed too. He is found guilty of murder and sent to prison. My sister would go into shock, have a nervous breakdown, and suffer from PTSD. Her two children at that time would live with us for a little while before living permanently with their dad's parents. Although my sister would get help and spend time in a treatment center, the damage from the event would haunt her for the remainder of her life. She'd have two more kids but would have to give them up for adoption due to mental instability.

She would remarry twelve years later. She and her husband would carry on as though they were happy, but he was extremely jealous and abusive. They would not seek any type of mental or physical health assistance. Although my sister was spiritually inclined and would quote bible verses often, she apparently didn't read the verses on wine or ignored them. *"Do not get drunk on wine, which leads to debauchery. Instead, be filled with the Spirit." (Ephesians 5:18).* Unfortunately, they weren't adhering to this scripture and alcohol abuse would lead to medical conditions that would take their lives in 2009 and 2010.

In August 1991, two of my nephews and one of their best friends, all just graduated from high school, were drinking with an older guy who had recently moved to town from Baltimore, Md. Their best friend had met the guy previously in the DC area. The older guy, in his mid-20's, was a convicted felon who came down to live with his grandmother. They all were discussing travels to DC, Baltimore, and New York. Neither of them had money or a vehicle. The felon informed them that he knows how to get transportation. See, he had some **gang affiliations** and knew how to do numerous crimes such as carjacking patrons. He attempted to carjack someone on a small highway that ran through town but was unsuccessful. My nephews and friend knew then that this guy is crazy, but they were fascinated by his boldness and wildness.

A few hours later, they all would meet up at the park and walk a mile or so to the only convenience store open that time of the night to purchase some more beer. The felon would tell them to wait on the corner while he goes in to get the beer.

While in the store, he pulls out a pistol and robs the store. (**Robbery**). There's only $78 in the cash register. The clerk and his roommate were in the store. He escorts them out the door to their car and makes them get in the front seat with the gun pointed at them. They drive around to the corner and he tells my nephews and friend to get in the car and don't say a word. Then, they drive off. (**Kidnapping**). He informs my nephews and best friend that they now have transportation. So, are the clerk and his roommate going with them, they thought. Are we going now? "We don't have any clothes," they'd say. The felon would inform them that they had to go now because the police were looking for him. He'd say that he and his girlfriend got in a fight earlier and she called the police.

After driving approximately eight miles outside of town, they would stop on the side of the road. The felon would say that he needs to take a leak and would summon the kidnapped victims out too. He'd take the keys with him. They would walk 80yds or so into the woods. A couple minutes later, my nephews and best friend would hear two, gun shots. The felon would come back to the car and tell one of the nephews to drive off. He'd say to them, *"I killed them mother fuckers and there are no witnesses to talk, right."* (**Murder**). **Can you say knocked off balance! Senseless!** Shocked and in fear, my nephews wouldn't say a word for a while. The felon would tell

them, *"don't worry, you all are safe as long as you keep quiet."*
Then off to Maryland they would go. They'd reach their
destination early the next morning.

When people commit to living on the wild side, are they
completely aware of the consequences? My nephews and best
friend were mesmerized by this guy's boldness. He took it as
though he now has some friends that he may be able to
manipulate. They were wanting that toughness and wild
approach, but they were not expecting all of this. *"For those
who guide these people are leading them astray; and those
who are guided by them are brought to confusion." (Isiah
9:16).* Now, they're facing robbery, kidnapping, stolen vehicle,
and accessory to murder. Wow!

While in Maryland, they would spend the day at the
felon's mom house. They would try to act as though nothing
happened, but they were obviously nervous. The next day, the
felon would tell them that they can go. The best friend would
call his brother who lived in DC to pick them up. Several days
later, they would get a ride back to NC. They'd take a day to
collaborate their thoughts and then go turn themselves into the
police. A retired army pilot, out looking for his lost dog, had
discovered the two bodies a day prior. The felon would be
arrested a couple days later in Maryland and extradited to NC to
face multiple charges including murder. My nephews and best

friend would be convicted a year later of first degree kidnapping with a 10-year sentence. The effects of the events would change many people's course of life. Family members and friends of the victims would never see their loved one's again. Nephews and best friend would spend their youthful years in prison when they should have been in college, working, in the military, and or starting their adult lives. Instead of the felon rehabilitating himself from prior charges, he would spend the rest of his life in prison and possibly put to death.

The nephews and their best friend would serve their time in prison. After getting released, nephews grow impatient with getting jobs and money. So, they would dibble and dab in petty drug dealing for a few years before being arrested again. The best friend would work small jobs just to stay busy. In the 10 years of imprisonment, each learned some trades but haven't put them to good use. All said that they read the bible often but didn't become faithful followers. Today, all of them are working but can't seem to find any stability or gratification. *"For I know the plans I have for you," declares the Lord, plans to prosper you and not harm you, plans to give you hope and a future. Then you will call on me and come and pray to me, and I will listen to you. You will seek me and find me, when you seek me with all your heart." (Jeremiah 29:11-13).*

Recently, one of my brothers got a chance to speak to

the father and sister of one of the victims. The father, a minister of a local church, told him that he struggled with his son's death for a long time. He had a lot of built up anger towards the man who killed his son and the guys who were with him. He said, *"How could someone be so evil to take someone's life on such a senseless act?" "My son was a child of God." "How could God allow this to happen?"* The minister finally realized that, to find peace and press forward, he had to forgive and let God handle the men lives. He'd continue to pray and ask God to continue walking with him and his family and guiding them. He'd include forgiveness in some of his sermons with his congregation. *"For if you forgive other people when they sin against you, your heavenly Father will also forgive you of your sins. But if you do not forgive those of their sins, then the Father will not forgive you of your sins." (Matthew 6:14-15).*

When my sister was shot by a policeman in 1975, it was enough to put the community in an uproar. She was handcuffed, put in the police car, then taken to the local hospital. Mom was called to the hospital. Belligerent and tearful, she asks the officer "why did you shoot her." He responded, "ma'am, she resisted arrest and struck an officer." Did she have a weapon or put your life in danger, she asked? No ma'am. Wow! Luckily, it wasn't a big news report. The officer felt justified in his shooting because he stated that she pushed and kicked him. Did that warrant him firing his gun and shooting her in the back? He could have killed her. He could have run her down and apprehended her easily, right. Was his life in jeopardy? Was she about to take someone's life? Was he trained to shoot first and apprehend afterwards? How was that justifiable? Small riots, gas bombings, and curfews would ensue from the event.

Mom was livid over the excuses and accusations from the police department and city officials. Our small branch of the **NAACP** couldn't gather the support for a major case against the police department. Furthermore, my sister and mom didn't want it to become a major case, but they wanted **Justice**. Mom couldn't afford a good attorney. The only attorney to step forward and offer help seemed to appease both sides. The officer would be suspended for several weeks and instructed to attend more training on dealing with non-life-threatening cases. Excited about the money, my sister would accept a small settlement from the city to drop the case. That little settlement would not take away the physical and mental scars that my sister would endure for the rest of her life. You see, the city nor the attorney agreed to pay for any psychological counseling for which my sister could have used. My sister would use the money for rent, furniture, clothes, food, etc. She would also use some of it to party, drink, and abuse drugs. Before she knew it, that little money was gone but the effects from the event were still present. The remainder of her life would be a roller coaster. She'd work on and off with a catering company at the Rockingham Motor Speedway. Her physical conditions from a childhood injury to her left shoulder plus getting shot in the same area would limit her work abilities.

The stress and disappointments would lead to more drug and alcohol abuse. Although she was the life of the party in the family, the abuse and scars would lead to medical conditions that would eventually take her life. She had just started attending church again prior to her death. She realized that she needed God in her life. Not only for herself but for her loved ones too. *"For to this you have been called, because Christ also suffered for you, leaving you an example, so that you might follow in his steps."* (1 Peter 2:21).

One of my best friends, Alonzo, was a victim in the Fort Hood, Texas terrorist attack in 2009. Forty-four people were shot, and 13 people were killed that day. He wasn't killed but he was shot several times. He credits his size and physical strength (6'9 and 325lbs) for his life. He was a staff sergeant with the medical unit and was on a temporary detachment. The shooting happened at the Soldier Readiness Center where soldiers would get treatment prior to deployment. Alonzo knew the attacker but never imagined that he would do the unthinkable. He stated that he was checking people in and stood approximately 8-10 feet away from Hasan, the shooter, moments before he shouted, *"Allahu Akbar"* then opened fire.

Allahu Akbar is an Islamic phrase that means Allah is the greatest. Was Allah the God in Hasan's mind? If so, this was not what God would have him do. If murderers state that they are doing the work of God, then they have truly been corrupted by Satan disguised as God. *"Do not be deceived, God is not mocked, for whatever one sows, that he will also reap. For the one who sows to his own flesh will from the flesh reap corruption, but the one who sows to the Spirit will from the Spirit reap eternal life." (Galatians 6:7-8)*.

Hasan began shooting in a sweeping motion at all military personnel in site. Several soldiers would charge at him, but they would be shot and killed. Alonzo would get shot in the abdomen, torso, and the left side of his head. **Can you say knocked off balance!** Of course, this unexpected, tragic event affected many families and changed their course of life. The shooting left Alonzo blind in one eye for a while. His rehabilitation would take nearly a year. Plus, he would endure Post Traumatic Stress(**PTSD**).

In multiple interviews, Alonzo has said that God wasn't ready for him to come home. He continues to find strength in prayer and rehabilitation. Although his course of life has

153

changed, he believes that his calling has been prepared. Since the rehab, Alonzo has gotten back to what he loves the most-helping people, coaching sports, spending time with his family, and thanking God. He says that the event continues to haunt him at times, but he knows that he must keep it moving. He also stated that he had to face his fears head on. Following his recovery, he had been walking in fear-constantly on alert for the unknown. He was avoiding large crowds. He realized that he's too much of a man to walk in fear. He also states that he is armed everywhere he goes now. His weapon(s) are concealed but he has a permit and a right to carry.

As a dear friend of Alonzo, I am a little bothered by his armed and ready mentality. I understand the "I'm too much of a man to walk in fear" part, but the weapons don't make you a strong man. *"Even though I walk through the valley of a shadow of death, I will fear no evil, for you are with me; your rod and your staff, they comfort me." (Psalm 23:4).* In many conversations, he speaks about guns. His Facebook profile shows guns. He posts things about guns. People kill people. It's the guns that add to that. I pray that his mental state keeps improving.

Today, Alonzo is an assistant basketball coach at a small college in Fayetteville, NC. He travels around the country speaking to high schoolers, future soldiers, and athletes. He encourages them on serving society, becoming good men and women of faith, being humble, and showing strength for yourself and the people around you. He's also an advocate for soldiers who suffer from PTSD from their war experiences. Above all, Alonzo is a strong believer in God, the father almighty. He prays and gives thanks to him every day for the strength, healing, and guidance he been given. *"And after you have suffered a little while, the God of all grace, who has called you to his eternal glory in Christ, will himself restore, confirm, strengthen, and establish you." (1 Peter 5:10).*

How do we control the senseless acts of gun violence? Is our government passing the appropriate laws and bills to improve the gun violence; or, are they enhancing the potential violence? How do you feel about the right to carry laws? Do you agree with citizens being able to purchase assault rifles? *Forbes.com* reported that gun sales skyrocketed by 158% since President Obama took office in 2008. A large proportion of those sales were assault weapons. Many owners have purchased bump stocks to go with those assault weapons for more rapid fire. **Wow! Why?** Were they preparing for another civil war?

Now, the **NRA** says that bump stocks should have special regulations. **Really!** What about regulating that no one can purchase assault weapons and or bump stocks! Why is it so easy to purchase assault weapons in our country? Is it because of money and kickbacks? (**Greed**). Is it the freedoms we have in America? Or, is our government and the NRA contending that it's a **2nd Amendment** right, but doesn't specify what kind of gun you can have or not have? What other countries have gun control laws like ours? Are we so proud to stand out from the rest? As these senseless acts continue to occur with assault weapons, we are mourning the deaths and talking about the acts, but doing nothing to curtail the weapons. Yeah, we all know that people are killing people not the weapons, but assault weapons allow little to no time to react.

How do we really keep guns off the streets and or from hands of the mentally disturbed? How do we combat the terrorist attacks? How can we minimize the gun violence associated with hatred? Do the people who commit these attacks really think they are following the advice of a higher power? Or, have their minds been infiltrated by Satan disguised as the Almighty? Gun violence has become one of the biggest issues in our country. Senseless acts have taken many lives. It appears that we take one step forward and two steps back on gun control. Too many guns are getting into the wrong hands. Many gun owners are purchasing weapons for the wrong reasons. Fear, hate, ignorance, gang activity, and mental instability have provoked a frenzy of gun violence that has knocked families and communities off balance. *"The Lord tests the righteous, but his soul hates the wicked and the one who loves violence." (Psalm 11:5).*

Chapter 11

Poverty (Generational, Choice, Situational)

There are many reasons for poverty in America. Oftentimes, it's geographical, socio-economic status, **generational**, health, and education. Many people who lose their jobs may experience **situational** poverty. Many victims of abuse in a relationship or marriage are subjected to poverty because they leave the home and struggle to make it on their own. Military veterans who suffer from depression or PTSD from war related incidents are also subjected to poverty and homeless. Many of their family members can't deal with their mental state and they are forced to live on their own without proper help from the government. Of course, there are many other reasons as well but one that I struggle to understand is **choice**.

Generational

Although mom grew up in poverty, she did not envision a poverty-stricken adult life. She realized that neither she nor her husband came from financially stable families, but their parents were hard working, loving, and caring people who had all the necessities. Also, it was a plus that they believed in Jesus

158

Christ. Mom was old-fashion and believed that the man of the house would work to provide for the family while the woman would stay home and take care of everything else. This was what the **Proverbs 31** woman was doing, right. This was not uncommon in those days. So, how does some offspring from families not follow those same values and or try to make a better life for themselves and their future families?

Mom and Mr. Scott didn't have anything more than a grammar school education. Nevertheless, they had good health, opportunities, and physical abilities. The babies started coming as soon as they were married, and mom couldn't do any outside work. But, there was plenty of work available for Mr. Scott. Unfortunately, he didn't want to work. So, how do you provide food, clothing, and shelter for your family. Although he was spoiled by his parents, they were not wealthy or financially comfortable enough to support him and his family. Mr. Scott was money hungry but didn't have the work ethic to make all that he could. I don't believe mom would have minded if he was always at work and bringing home the money for the family. She would have realized that the financial support gives the family some stability and comfort. Unfortunately, that didn't come close to happening.

Even when Mr. Scott was at home, there were only the bare necessities for the family. To think of anything extra was

absurd. If he made any extra money, it was used for his
womanizing flings. When the older kids got paid for working in
the fields, he would even spend some of their earned money on
his transgressions. When he abandoned the family for good, he
left them unprotected and with nothing. There was minimal
food, no money, rent due the next month, no transportation,
and no emotional support. **Can you say knocked off balance!**
What happened to the man, the husband, the father, the
provider, and the child of God? *"But if anyone does not
provide for his relatives, and especially for members of his
household, he has denied the faith and is worse than an
unbeliever." (1 Timothy 5:8)*.

   After Mr. Scott left, mom had to figure out how she was
going to survive and take care of twelve kids. The oldest child
was fourteen and the youngest was less than a year old. She
explained to the older two boys, age thirteen and eleven, that
they would have to continue to work in the cotton fields to help
support the family. The twelve-year-old daughter would work
in the fields as well, but she became an emotional wreck due to
daddy's abandonment and would require some treatment. The
oldest child would stay at home and help mom with the
younger siblings while mom sought help. There was no **Peter
(financial or church establishment) to rob but Paul (landlord's
rent)** still needed to be paid. Mom would beg her siblings for

help. They managed to give her a little money for food but couldn't afford to pay her rent. A couple of the brothers, who lived in Rochester, NY, would come and bring her boxes of clothes and food for the kids.

Mom appreciated all that her family and friends did for them. She continued to pray and ask for guidance and support. A few months later, it was the winter months and there was no farm work for the boys. Mom had exhausted all financial support from family and friends. The electricity in the house is disconnected. No lights, food spoiling in the refrigerator, and no electric stove to cook on. The landlord comes by and informs mom that she is two months behind on rent and if not paid in full within the next 2 weeks, she would have to leave. Mom only had $150 but she needed $400.

One day, mom had been gone for hours trying to find friends and family to borrow money from. Several of the younger siblings were crying because they were hungry. With no electricity to cook on the stove, the oldest sister went outside and dug a hole in the back yard, place leaves and twigs in it to make a fire, and boiled some rice and fried some chicken for her siblings. **Wow! Can you say creativity and survival!** *"And he lifted his eyes on his disciples, and said, "blessed are you who are poor, for yours is the kingdom of God." "Blessed are you who are hungry now, for you shall be satisfied."*

"Blessed are you who weep now, for you shall laugh." (Luke 6:20-21).

Within that two weeks, mom would receive government assistance in the form of food vouchers but that would not pay the rent. A small welfare check would come a month or so later. So, she would use $100 to pay a deposit for a 3-bedroom house to rent in the Dobbins Heights area of Hamlet. She'd use the other $50 to pay a deposit on electricity. There was no electric heat, so they would use a wood burning stove and a small kerosene heater. She would use the food vouchers to go and buy food. Content for now, mom wouldn't worry about how to pay next month's rent and utility bills. She would pray for increase.

While shopping with the vouchers, the county welfare office monitored the use of the vouchers. They sent a representative to pick mom up from home and take her to the grocery store with the voucher and ensure she was not buying any junk food such as: potato chips, candy, soda pops, and cookies or cakes. Only milk, bread, cereal, meat, fruit, vegetables, cooking oil, flour, one bag of sugar, and grains were to be purchased. Although mom despised being monitored, she was thankful that she had a place to live and food for the kids. *"If we have food and covering, with these we shall be content." (1 Timothy 6:8).* Besides, she was a great cook and she could bake homemade cakes and pies. Plus, she'd cut up potatoes and make French fries.

Mom would also receive a form of **Medicaid** to help with medical coverage for her and the kids. That was much needed because it would cover the expenses for her son's diabetes and dental and medical check-ups for the other kids. Now, the biggest challenge was getting them to the doctor for check-ups. Due to the lack of transportation, many doctor visits were canceled unless there was something severe with one of the kids.

As years passed, mom would continue to struggle to get financial support. The lack of money for rent would force her to move the family many times. A couple of the homes were dilapidated, insect, and rodent infested. Most had no bathrooms. There were **outhouses** in the backyards. They did have running water, but bathing was done in **wash pots**. Outhouses were not completely uncommon in the 60's but many households had advanced to bathrooms. Oftentimes, the siblings would spend a lot of time with their friends and use their bathroom to avoid using the outhouse. Their friends didn't seem to mind because they were cool friends to be around.

As you recall, I am the last of the sixteen children. Although things improved during my childhood, we were still in poverty, the younger three kids didn't experience as much as the others. It was difficult moving from the projects with clean bathrooms, central heat and air to a dilapidated home with an outhouse, no bathroom, kerosene and wood burning heat, and fans and portable ac units in the windows. Nevertheless, we learned to be humble. We still didn't have much, but we had love and the basics. We didn't miss much school. We were healthy, smart, and had plenty of friends. Of course, the older siblings would say that we were spoiled-especially me and mom would go the extra mile for us. I don't think I was much different than many other youngest children from families, right.

We endured some ridicule and talking behind our backs at school because of our clothing but not enough to change our behaviors or provoke fights. We were the hand-me-down kings for several years until we reach our teenage years and growth spurts started occurring. I would say that the most embarrassing thing for us was that we only had two pairs of shoes. I had one for everyday wear and one for special occasions. Of course, we were growing boys and those shoes would become too tight within months. One year, while in high school, money was tight, and I needed a pair of basketball shoes for the games-sound familiar. I couldn't get my dad to buy them for me and I was too ashamed to ask the coach. I was the star player on the team; surely, he would have bought me a pair. Nevertheless, a good friend on the JV team who considered me a **role model**, let me wear his shoes for half the season. **Wow!** Thank you, Kevin Martin!

Choice

By the late 60's, several siblings had moved out and started their own families. That was good for mom because there were less kids to take care of. She is now in a relationship with a married man, but he is helping her pay rent. They have a couple of kids together so that is the least that he could do. A few of the older kids are acting out to get attention. They have become disobedient, staying out late with friends, smoking, drinking, skipping school, experimenting with drugs, and engaging in sexual intercourse. Although mom is trying to be a disciplinarian, she is a little overwhelmed and can't control them all. She prays for their well-being and **choices** and asks God to look over them.

Several of the kids were torn between going to school, hanging out in the streets, or quitting school and working in the fields. Although quitting school was not the best option, that's exactly what a couple brothers done. They didn't realize that a good **education** would assist them on getting out of poverty. As the 70's approached, two of the sisters could have used some fatherly advice to let them know what their so-called boyfriends were after. Unfortunately, there was no father around and the boyfriends would get what they wanted, impregnate our sisters, and leave them. Now, they're left raising a child on their own as a teenager; plus, being judged by others. Mom would feel like a hypocrite when telling her daughters about *abstaining from sexual immorality and controlling their lustful tendencies. (Thessalonians 4:3-5).*

One brother would get caught up with the wrong kind of friends who were trying to make money the wrong way. They would grow jealous of what some of the kids at school had and would result to stealing and selling the merchandise for money. This activity would lead him in and out of juvenile camps, but he'd continue the same activities upon release. Another brother would become a wanderer-traveling up and down the east coast living with relatives and trying to find work to avoid going to school.

The thirteenth child, feeling like somewhat of an outcast, would act out by skipping school and going somewhere to be alone-feeling as though he is not loved the same as others. Satan's deception is real. *"God speaks, that he created every part of us, that he placed us in our mom's womb. He praises that you are to be feared, that all you do may be*

different but in his heart, you are loved. (Psalms 139:13-14).
He was very smart in school, but he just didn't want to go.
Because he was intelligent and had a very mature stature, he'd
deceive grocery store and movie theater employers about his
age to get a job. He was twelve but looked as though he was
sixteen or seven. Mom compromised with him. She told him
that she would not blow the whistle on him if he'd go to school
and keep truancy officers from harassing her. He agreed and
went back to school. The job made him feel needed,
responsible, and independent. Now, he could help himself and
provide some support for the family.

When we moved into the 5-bedroom house in the
projects, one of mom's true friends moved there as well. She
had a large family too (11) and they got the 2nd largest home in
the projects which was a 4-bedroom house. Mom had told me
that they both had prayed about getting out of the dilapidated
homes that they lived in. They'd spend time at each other's
houses and share recipe's and scriptures. They'd discuss how
the homes would give their kids stability and hopes of going to
school regularly and getting a good education. Mom and her
friend both had sons who were extremely gifted in football and
basketball. Both sons were on track to become potential all-
state athletes and potential college material in their perspective
sport.

Unfortunately, my brother would use the excuse of being embarrassed and ridiculed about his clothes and not having a pair of good basketball shoes as reasons to quit school. **Hmmm....** Now, as good as he was, someone would have bought him a pair of basketball shoes. Although that was a big piece of the puzzle, it was not the true reason for his embarrassment. Like a few other older siblings, our brother had a learning disability and struggled to learn at the same pace as others in his class. By the 9th grade, he was already 2 grade levels behind. Only one teacher and the sister next to him realized his learning deficiencies. That was the real, underlying reason that he quit. **Wow!** *In Mark 8:14-18, Jesus references that the disciples were slow learners, that sometimes they didn't quite understand his words. If I'm not mistaken, the disciples turned out to be well respected men.*

I'm not a psychiatrist, but I realize that when someone is constantly ridiculed for being slow, they start to believe they are. It becomes difficult to find friends because those friends don't want to be labeled too. They don't realize that they have a condition that follows generational poverty. They become ashamed and embarrassed around others. They tend to shut down, go into seclusion, avoid people and situations, and quit activities. Did you know that the learning disability could be directly related to the poverty? Studies have shown that children who are nutritionally challenged, living in a poor environment, restless, etc. can't focus well in school. The conditions affect they brain and cognitive learning.

There's a poverty series titled *"Understanding and Working with Students and Adults from Poverty" written by Ruby K. Payne, PH.D.* which describes eight key resources that influence achievement.

1. **Money** is the number one element. 2. Being able to control one's **emotional** responses-especially in negative situations without engaging in self-destructive behaviors. 3. **Mentally** possessing the intellectual ability and acquired skills to write, read, comprehend, and count. 4. Being **spiritually** inclined in divine purpose and guidance. 5. Being **physically** healthy and mobile. 6. Having a **support system** with family and friends as a backup resource. 7. Having **role models** to look up to, who are appropriate and caring. Plus, one's who are not engaged in destructive behaviors. 8. **Having knowledge of unspoken cues and habits** of a group-such as middle class. Of course, most if not all these key resources are absent with those growing up in poverty.

Here are some more known facts about poverty:

- Poverty is both a cause and a consequence of **poor health**. (*www.healthpovertyaction.org*).
- It's a vicious circle where both poverty seems linked to greater rates of **mental illness**, and in some cases, certain kinds of mental illness seem linked to a greater likelihood of living in poverty. *(psychcentral.com).*
- Children who experience poverty during their preschool and early school years are more susceptible to

dropping out of school than children and adolescents who experience poverty only in later years.

- The stresses of poverty may impair **learning ability** in young children.
- Many children in poverty develops low self-esteem
- **Poverty** is both a cause and a consequence of **teen pregnancy** and childbearing. Two-thirds of young unmarried mothers are poor and around 25 percent go on **welfare** within three years of a child's birth. Low educational attainment among **teen** mothers affects their economic opportunities and earnings in later years. (www.ncsl.org).
- There's a direct connection with substance abuse and child abuse (physical, emotional, sexual) due to poverty. *(www.treatmentsolutions.com)*
- Inequality, segregation, poverty, and lack of mental health resources accounts for a lot of gun violence in America. *(salon.com)*.
- Many young men who grow up in poverty are at a higher risk to become affiliated with gang activity-especially if there is poor success in school. They feel a sense of belonging, power, control, and prestige. *(trauma.blog.yorku.ca)*.
- The **cycle of poverty** can continue for generations without drive, goals, education, support, and outside help and influence.

Can you see how these missing resources affect families who grow up in poverty? How are you handling it today? Mom was spiritually inclined, but she lacked the support to help guide her kids on that path. Most of them were physically healthy but didn't have the mobility to get to and from places they needed to go, even school. All other resources were absent, and you could see how our family was affected by it. Some of Dr.

Payne's literature describes how most school systems are structured on middle-class hidden rules and kids growing up in poverty struggle to understand those rules. Today, some of her work has been adopted in many school systems to help prepare and train educators on how to deal with students who are growing up in poverty. Her literally work is astonishing. I'd recommend that you read some of it when you get a chance. It describes some true, hard facts of behaviors related to poverty.

All these occurrences are attributed to poverty, lack of guidance, and being unprotected. We weren't neglected by mom but some of us were very impatient with our current situations and wanted immediate change. *"The plans of the diligent lead surely to abundance, but everyone who is hasty comes only to poverty." (Proverbs 21:5).* Regardless of what politicians, educators, and lobbyist say about poverty-stricken families, the playing fields are uneven for many of us. We don't get the same opportunities because of our income level, education, and or environment. The probability of us making it to a middle-class level or better is extremely low. When we are given a **choice** and opportunity for a good education and or job, we must give it our all. Otherwise, we're going to fall into the same vicious circle. Can you relate to this? How has growing up in poverty affected your livelihood? Are you out of poverty? If not, why? If so, how have you prevailed? What is keeping you at this level? Are you there by choice?

Mom's best friend's youngest son made a choice to stay in school. He surrounded himself with positive friends. He would become one of the top high school football receivers in NC. He would lead his team to their first state championship. He was given a full athletic scholarship to attend NC State University where he would become an All ACC player. He was drafted by the Philadelphia Eagles in 1982 and blossomed into one of the top receivers in the NFL. He made the Pro Bowl five times. He would go on to have a 9-year career with the Eagles.

Today, he is a radio analyst with the Eagles. He spent several years hosting a free football clinic for youth in our home town. He and several other players from Hamlet donated money to open a basketball gym and rebuild one of our local parks. He also spends time in the Boys and Girls clubs in the New Jersey and the Philadelphia area mentoring kids on the importance of education and giving back to their communities. He talks to them about being humble, staying away from drugs and alcohol, peer pressure, and saying "no". Well done, Mike Quick!

Although our brother, Steve, used excuses to quit school, he did get a job and maintained it. He would go on to become the first son to get married, buy his own home, and move from poverty to middle-class status. He and his wife didn't have any kids, but they helped mentor and raise several nieces and nephews. They'd also give resources and guidance to brothers, sisters, and cousins to help them get on their feet, so to speak. Though Steve and his wife weren't the most spiritual couple, they would still encourage them to **pray** and stay humble. Several of them would complete high school, enter college, military, and land good jobs. Steve would also go on to work for the same employer for 40 years. In March of 2014, he became the first sibling to retire from his job. Mom would have been very proud of him.

Situational

Remember the thirteenth child! Well, he would continue working at the movie theater and grocery store, but he'd quit school after turning sixteen. A couple years later, he would migrate to New Jersey. While there, he would go back to school and get his GED. He would continue his education in trade schools, earning certificates in electrical, pneumatics, boiler operations, and auto mechanics. By the age of 21, he would land a good job as a boiler room operator with the city of Camden and eventually the controller. A year or so later, he'd meet the love of his life, get married, and start a family. He would become financially stable and would send mom money occasionally. What a gratifying feeling for him, especially for someone who once felt like an outcast. Good job brother!

Unfortunately, ten years later, he and his family would fall victims to situational poverty. Unable to balance work, stress, children, and different stages of the marriage, he and his wife would fuss and fight. She'd grow jealous of his fondness from neighbors and friends. Although **submissive**, she'd began to feel as though she was not contributing enough. They'd try to cope with the stress through drugs, alcohol, adultery, etc. One big piece missing in their lives, like many others even my life, was faith and walk with God or that higher power. Because it went missing, Satan stepped in. *"Let us walk with decency, as in the daylight; not in carousing and drunkenness, not in the sexual impurity and promiscuity, not in quarrelling and jealousy. (Romans 13:13).*

Satan's wrath would cause my brother and his wife to become addicted to drugs. They would go into **debt, lose his job,** be evicted from their house, and separate. **Wow! Can you say knocked off balance!** Their course of life has truly changed. His wife would take their 3 kids and move back to her home town in NC and he would move in with our sister. Not able to wing himself from the drugs, he would have to leave my sister's place. He would become homeless and spend time in and out of jail due to child support. He and his wife would eventually divorce. Today, they both are continuing to struggle with their lives. He is so hung up on past events and can't seem to move forward. Year after year, it's one step forward and two steps back. **Can you relate?**

I recall my brother joining the Muslim faith and speaking highly of Allah during his marriage. I'm not sure how his faith was rolled out to his wife and kids. We, his immediate family, constantly encourage him to take small steps to bounce back. The three youngest boys often told him how we use to look up to him (**role model**) because of his intellect, hard work, and providing behaviors. He still has those traits, but he becomes offensive and feels harassed when we talk about them. **Satan will not let go that easily.** Nevertheless, it's never too late to pick yourself up. Pray! Walk with God, Allah, or whomever may be your higher power! We are not placed on this earth to have a selfish purpose. Furthermore, he has kids and grandkids who need some guidance. He could be very instrumental in helping them break the generational cycle of poverty and possibly not fall victims of situational poverty too.

As mentioned earlier in mom's story, several of her kids would get good educations. Her last three girls and the last three boys would go on to graduate from high school. Several would go on to college and earn Bachelor's Degrees. One sister would continue her education earning a Master's degree in Education. Currently, she teaches **Autistic** kids and has been named Teacher of the year. She is well respected in her school district and one of the top educators. Another brother is a guidance counselor in the local school system and is earning his stripes as well. Several siblings have gone back to school and received their GED's and held some very nice jobs. And now, here I am writing a book. Mom was proud of all before she passed away. She would be ecstatic about the book. Little does she know, she is assisting me with it.

Despite growing up in poverty, mom tried her best to promote faith, unity, education, discipline, instruction, and perseverance with her kids. She was hoping that the generational cycle of poverty would slowly diminish with her grandkids and so on. Of course, she realized that the deck was stacked against them all. She was doing it alone except with God's help. Not only was she and the kids left unprotected, they were left unequipped. Mr. Scott was not around to give his kids the basic tools for life. There was no instruction or guidance from him. It was obvious that Satan's corruption obstructed his mindset. *"All scripture is breathed out by God and profitable for teaching, for reproof, for correction, and for training in righteousness, that the man of God may be competent, equipped for every good work. (2 Timothy 3:16-17).* Mom was spiritually equipped and did a pretty good job of teaching those values. Unfortunately, she was unprotected, and Satan kept tugging.

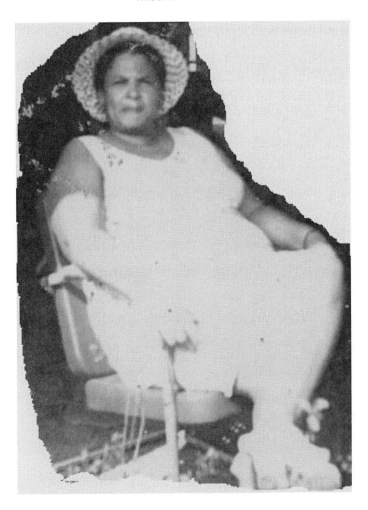

Although none of mom's kids have made it beyond middle-class, only a few have continued to live in poverty. The reasons have been health issues, poor choices, loss of jobs, contentment, and fear. Many family members use the excuse of staying around to take care of their mothers, fathers, brothers, sisters, etc. to remain in poverty. We all are hoping that the generational cycle is broken soon. We must continue to teach our children to walk a narrow path, believe, and trust in God. *"The Lord shall increase you more and more, you and your children." (Psalms 115:14).*

Today, there are nine siblings living. Five live in NC, three in NJ, and myself, in TN. Despite the distance, we are a close-knit family. We get together every Thanksgiving and sometimes other holidays throughout the year. It's a time to enjoy each other's company. We eat, gossip, listen to music, sing, dance, play games, cards, and more. Although it doesn't seem like much, it's a time for us to reflect on the importance of family, support, love, and fun. Of course, mom enjoyed those times too. Regardless of our circumstances, mom encouraged us to spend as much time as possible with each other and be grateful for what we have. *"Finally, all of you, have unity of mind, sympathy, brotherly love, a tender heart, and a humble mind." (1 Peter 3:8).*

Did you grow up in poverty? How have you progressed? Are you content with your current situation? Are there opportunities to press forward and break the generational cycle? How is your situation affecting your kids? Were you and your kids left unprotected like our mother? Are they properly equipped? Are you allowing the environment or community to educate your kids? Do you feel as though teachers are responsible for controlling the behaviors and equipping your kids? If so, why? Are you using negativity, inequalities, and poor choices as an excuse to remain in poverty? Have you been hit with situational poverty? How are you handling the blow? Are you driven with short and long-term goals to remove yourself from the situation? Are you praying and asking God or a higher power for guidance?

Chapter 12

Work Stress

While some workplace stress is normal, excessive stress can interfere with your productivity and performance, impact your emotional health, affect your relationships and home life. It can even mean the difference between success and failure on the job. *(HelpGuide.org).* Undoubtedly, work stress could cause potential damage to your livelihood. It can **knock you off balance and change your course of life**.

There are certain professions that may carry a heavier burden of stress than others. Often, we hear people state that they have one of the most stressful jobs in the world. Of course, most jobs carry their own type of stress. What is it that makes your job so stressful? Is it the environment, the people, the workload, or the job itself? Are you creating the stress yourself by what you are doing or not doing? Before you become overwhelmed with the work stress and begin to make some poor choices, can you just find a job that's less stressful? Many people decide to endure the stress, creating physical and mental health concerns, abusing drugs and alcohol, neglecting or abusing their families, constant anger, etc. The thing that we don't want to see happen to stressed out workers is someone

"Going Postal".

Here are *Forbes and Salary.com's* Top 10 Most Stressful Jobs in the U.S:

1. **Enlisted Military Personnel**. This job involves thorough training and skill set. Going to war in foreign countries! It's one that you can kill or be killed. Witnessing traumatic events! Possibility of battling PTSD amongst other things.
2. **Surgeons**. Although highly trained, they are cutting someone open to repair, remove, or put stuff in your body. One bad move could be life-threatening.
3. **Firefighter**. Running into fire and rescuing people in dire straits! Conditions are hazardous and dangerous to everyone's health.
4. **Airline Pilot**. Soaring miles above the earth and traveling at speeds over 500 miles per hour with hundreds of people entrusting you with their lives.
5. **Police Officers**. Putting your life on the line every time you go to work. Called to situations that you never know what to expect.
6. **Registered Nurse-ER**. They are the link between the patients and the doctors. Trying to determine who is priority when there's a chaotic trauma room with gunshot victims, blood, body fluids, etc.
7. **911-Emergency Dispatcher**. You may not think of this job being stressful but EMS, police, firefighters, etc. only get to where there going because of the dispatcher.
8. **News reporter**. Stories must be told. Long hours covering trials, meetings, breaking news, follow-ups, and calls in the middle of the night.
9. **Social Worker**. My brother used to tell me how stressed he was at work. I didn't quite understand

until he explained it to me. Being placed into emergency situations where potential abuse or violence is taking place and no one else wants to step up. So, it falls on you. Trying to advocate for those in dire straits, be understanding, and sympathetic as well.

10. **School Teacher**. When I was a young middle school student, the teachers didn't seem stressed or I wasn't paying attention. Most teachers are underpaid, they are working late grading papers or going over curriculums. Many are dealing with a large proportion of behavior issues with students yet trying to shape their minds. Failing them, endangers their futures.

Do you agree with these top stressful jobs? What stressful jobs not listed are at the top of your list? Can you imagine our society without the jobs? Wow! Never really thought about it much, right!

As an elementary school student, do you recall the teachers or your parents asking you *"What do you want to be when you grow up?"* How many of the titles listed above were mentioned by you or other students? For many of us, these jobs were related to what we saw in society or on TV. Of course, at a young age, we didn't know what stress was nor what these professions endured. Oddly enough, no one ever mentioned what kind of person you should strive to be in these professions. Without question, these jobs require special kind of people. In *Tony Dungy's book Uncommon Life*, he writes *"In our society the struggle between being and doing starts early and is often innocently encouraged. We ask our children what they want to be when they grow up much more often than what kind of person they want to be. It's a focus on what they do rather than who they are. And most will spend their lives identifying themselves by what they do."* Isn't that interesting?

Mr. Scott didn't work long enough to endure stress on the job. He didn't want to work at all. He was more stressed that he needed to work. We're not sure what he was striving for or what his vision was, but work wasn't it. It appeared that working in the fields where women worked also was exciting to him, but it didn't reap much money. When he landed that good job with the Seaboard Railroad, all the excited had ended. A real, structured job had begun. It was one of the top paying blue-collar jobs in the area. Plus, it would give a great benefit package after the 60-day probation period. The insurance coverage from the benefits would help with medicine for the son with Diabetes, exams for all, and medical costs. The salary from the job would be enough to maintain and support his family needs. Plus, overtime was plentiful, and he could make extra money for other items. Unfortunately, Mr. Scott didn't make it through the probationary period. He was leaving the house as though he was going to work but wasn't showing up. Mom thought he was at work. Eventually, he was fired.

Mr. Scott made a choice that he was not going to work.

In his mind, he didn't want to spend the rest of his life working to support his family. In fact, he never worked another real job in his life. When he abandoned mom and the kids, he realized that if his social security number is used for a job, that his check could be garnished by the state of NC for child support. So, he decided to be a hustler-only working jobs that paid him in cash. He never sent any money to mom for food, clothes, rent, or anything else. *"What good is it, my brothers, if someone says he has faith but does not have works? Can that faith save him? If a brother or sister is poorly clothed and lacking in daily food, and one of you says to them, "Go in peace, be warmed and filled," without giving them the things needed for the body, what good is that? So, also faith by itself, if it does not have works, is dead." (James 2:14-17).*

Mom never worked a real job either. It's not that she didn't want to, she just didn't have time. Plus, she was tired from child-bearing, anxiety, etc. Nevertheless, she put in countless hours caring for her kids and endured a lot of stress at home. That was her job. Although the work took a toll on her, she persevered. I believe mom would have been a great worker for someone. She had the work ethic and strength. With all the things she endured, work would have been a piece of cake.

Do you remember that job that came available two months prior to my divorce? Well, it was still available at the beginning of 2011 and I took it. Now, I am a department manager with 24-hour, 7 days a week responsibility of the area. Oftentimes, I would get calls in the middle of the night. The job was consuming a lot of my time. Fortunately, I was now separated from my wife, out of the house, and headed towards divorce. I wouldn't have been able to maintain this type of job and work on marital issues.

Although I had begun to date, it was difficult because of the mental and physical exhaustion from the job. My job was good and bad. See, I am now working a normal M-F schedule. Prior to that, I was working a twelve-hour rotation only having every other weekend off. It was helping with my recovery from the divorce and loneliness, but it was stressful. I was finding myself eating out a lot and drinking more and more alcohol. The next thing you know, I had gained 20lbs (***Poor Diet***) in less than a year.

Over the next year, I was being groomed by my Area Business manager as his potential replacement. He was retiring by the end of the year. That grooming was put to a halt because we had a new supervisor whom I needed help to train. That supervisor would report to me later. Then I had to fill in for another direct reports who was out on medical leave. All of this was being done while trying to do my job as well. By the end of the year, I had applied for my manager's job but I was turned down because I needed more experience and development. So, I was told. Plus, there was a manager coming in with a lot of business experience and he would help me grow. Ok, that's seems fine, right. Only, this manager had never been in this type of environment; furthermore, he had no knowledge of the area and had only delegated over the past 10 years. Our facility required more hands-on managers or at least seen by the teammates on every shift. For him, he could care less about who the teammates were or what they did. That was my job he thought, and his responsibility was the area business. Managing down was not his thing, so he would continue to delegate-primarily to me. He would not be able to help my development at all. In fact, I was assisting in his training. **Can you say knocked off balance!** I was a little upset, but my mentor and outgoing manager was livid that someone was brought in with no knowledge. My workload would become extremely heavy and my personal time was very short.

It appears my quality of life didn't seem to matter very much to him or upper management. Now, I'm over-looked and overwhelmed. I can't concentrate on my job because of the struggles with my direct report's shortcomings and medical issues. I am having to work some weekends because of their absences. My manager doesn't know anything about the area-yet the business. Instead of going to him for assistance, he's relying on me for all the decision making. **Hmmm... So, why is he the manager?** Oh, his job is to run the business for the area. My job is to handle all the day to day activities. **Wow! Really! Basically, he can't help me at all.** I'm beginning to plan my course of action.

Looking ahead, I'm seeing some potential **nepotism**, frustration, long hours, and a whole lot of stress. With that said, I felt as though I needed to reduce my stress and have a better quality of life. *"Commit to the Lord whatever you do, and he will establish your plans." (Proverbs 16:3).* So, in May of 2013, I decided to take a position with the company in NC. It was a lateral management move with a great chance to advance within a couple years. My new ABM was very experienced. He was excited to have me there and just as eager to develop me. My kids seemed to be doing well and I thought it would be nice to move back in my home state. Plus, I was close to my brothers and sisters. Now, I can hang out with them more and have some relaxing times too. My kids could spend summers and other days with me and possibly go to college in NC.

Well, the move and transition weren't going as smooth as I thought. It was exciting for the first seven months. I enjoyed going on fishing trips with friends and family, exploring the eastern NC area and beaches, attending local college sporting events (ECU, Duke, UNC, NC State), and meeting more beautiful women! A series of events would occur as I was adapting to the new work environment.

In late January of 2014, my best friend of 35 years would pass away from a **pulmonary embolism**. He was one that I could confide in when I needed to vent or get advice. My youngest son is diagnosed with **anxiety and depression**. Another dear friend, college basketball teammate, and former NBA player, Anthony Mason, would die from a heart condition. I had to administer disciplinary action to one of my direct reports that would force him to retire early. The company launched a new program that allowed the teammates to rate their managers on effectiveness, trust, relationships, etc. The ratings would show how much we were impacting morale in our areas. I would have the lowest rating in the building. Wow! I was **temporarily knocked off balance**. It was enough to alter my course of life.

I had become stressed again. My diet was poor, and I was not exercising. I would pull back on dinner dates. I began to go back and forth to Tennessee to be with my son as he battles depression! My best friend is gone, I don't have other friends like him to confide in, I'm in a new environment, and my teammates doesn't like what I'm doing. I'm feeling *stressed* and out of balance. *"Cast all your anxiety on him because he cares for you." (1 Peter 5:7)*.

My ratings were not based on my effectiveness as a leader. My direct reports and teammates were struggling to adapt to my management style. After observing and taking notes for the first 3 months, I could see through some of the **BS** in my department. I re-emphasized that everyone should be doing their jobs. I'd inform all that there would be no "I" in team and no favoritism. I'd also informed my direct reports(supervisors) that we will hold people accountable for under-achieving and producing abnormal products that get to our customers. There was an open-door policy for teammates to see HR and upper management if there was an issue with their supervisor or manager. Well I was bypassed, and had to explain my actions with the plant manager. Once clarity of my actions was communicated, I was supported.

I had to change some of my behaviors and approach. Of course, I didn't know that scripture (1 Peter 5:7), but I would pull myself together with some **prayer** and self-perseverance. My manager informed me that he had the utmost confidence in me and despite the ratings, the department was doing well. I would build better relationships with my team by listening and encouraging involvement from them. I would enter a leadership group in the community that praises teamwork and relationship building. Now, I have more friends and plenty of outside activities to consume my time. I would eat better and exercise at least three times a week. I would pray for my son and find ways to spend more time with him.

In the late summer of 2015, I moved back to Tennessee. I wanted to be in my youngest son's presence as he battled depression. I felt as though I could help him more. It seemed to have worked. He was super excited and moved in with me immediately. I was fortunate to transfer back to my previous location. I had to step down to a supervisor role instead of a manager but that was fine. I just needed to be back. I was blessed and humble with the opportunity to come back without leaving the company. Although I had desired to become a manager again, I've remained patient. *"Humble yourselves, therefore, under God's mighty hand, that he may lift you up in due time." (1 Peter 5:6).*

After returning, I realize that I am far more developed than several new managers in the facility. The production manager for the plant assured me that I would get an opportunity to move up soon if I desired to. Two Area Business Manager jobs came available within a year. I applied for them, but I was turned down again. Surely, I wasn't turned down because of education or experience, but there was not a real explanation other than "we decided to go with two other deserving guys." I couldn't disagree, but neither of the guys who got the jobs had a college degree and it was highly recommended. One of them was in school working towards his degree. The other guy had more supervisory experience than I did. There were rumors that the upper management in the plant was not going to give me an opportunity to get one of the jobs because they thought I ran away previously and didn't deserve it. **Wow!**

Those rumors made me feel some kind of way but I just let it be. I had only been back a year and I couldn't complain. Maybe the timing wasn't right for me. Nevertheless, my credentials are good. I have plenty of experience. I'm educated. I have a good rapport with team members and they trust me. You would think that I'm a prime candidate for one of these positions, right. Furthermore, there is very little diversity and no **people of color** in these positions. **Hmmm....** In my twenty-five years with the company, I've only seen one person of color in those positions at our facility and she was only passing through. **Does this Fortune 500 company realize this?**

In my opinion, this facility and the organization had two good opportunities to help themselves by promoting someone of color and one who was truly qualified. Plus, he is one of the facilities own and mentored by ABM's who were highly respected. It may have helped gain appreciation from teammates who expressed dislike for the upper management's hiring practices, possibly increase morale, and inspire others who were uncertain about applying for such positions because of the nepotistic ways over the years. What do you think? *"When a man's ways please the Lord, he makes even his enemies to be at peace with him." (Proverbs 16:7).*

As I am writing this book, would you believe that I report to that same manager who came in before I left for NC. He was in a different area of the plant when I returned. Ironically, he was struggling in that area too. He seemed very stressed and his job was in jeopardy. In my opinion, it appeared that his lack of knowledge and inability to influence, build trust, and develop others was leading to his failure. He wasn't the only manager struggling. Several others couldn't handle the pressure from the job or had become stressed. So, they either quit, were demoted, moved to another area, or place on special assignment. It's difficult to manage if you are not engaged and lack the ability to influence others.

Nevertheless, he was moved to the area where I am. That's interesting, isn't it! Maybe plant management was thinking that he could use my knowledge to his advantage and success. Now, I don't deserve to have an ABM job, but I can help him as much as possible. **Does this happen on your job?** I agreed to give him pointers and tips. On the other-hand, I informed him that I would not do his job. I'm not the only one who helps him, but he is truly comfortable when I'm there. He has a lot of confidence and trust in my knowledge of the area. Plus, he seems to need help with decision-making.

Today, he is trying harder and is more involved. Of course, the teammates would like to see him down on the floor more but he's not that kind of manager. He continues to rely heavily on me and others for information. Every now and then, I'm reluctant to help but I am a team player. *"Iron sharpens iron, and one man sharpens another." (Proverbs 27:17).* He applauds all of us for our efforts and tells us how much he appreciates our work. He also states that he doesn't know what he'd do without us.

Initially, I was a little disappointed about being turned down for the ABM jobs, but I didn't let it get me down. I remained humble for the opportunity to be back in Tennessee and around my son. Most of the teammates feel that I am out of place and should be an ABM. That makes me feel good. One major difference today is that I'm not stressed. I'm not taking any work home. I'm in a better place mentally and spiritually. I even have time to focus and write a book. I like that the teammates respect me and I also like that others look to me for information and guidance. **Hmmm….** It sounds as though I may have the ability to lead and develop others, huh. Although my company has been good to me and has given me some great opportunities, my desires to advance has now changed due to the nepotistic ways. Can you relate? *"For God shows no partiality." (Romans 2:11).*

Although there were other events contributing to my stress, work was at the top of the list. How is your stress level? Are you working a good, low stress job today? Are you able to multi-task on the job without creating stress? Can you handle the unexpected events without stressing yourself out? Is favoritism on the job causing you stress? Is the stress affecting your quality of life? How about your health? What are you doing about it?

Social Workers

One of my brother use to be a **social worker**. He left the position because of stress. He'd often talk about being physically and mentally exhausted from the week of work. There was one case that he had to investigate, and it pushed him over the top. A two-year boy had been hospitalized for suspected child abuse. The parents were separated and lived in different houses. The boy had been with his father for the weekend. The father normally would take the child back home on Sunday evening, so he could prepare for daycare. That weekend the father decided to keep the child and take him to daycare on Monday morning. The mother worked at the daycare and was fine with the decision.

The mother wasn't at work yet when the father dropped the child off. Upon feeding him breakfast, another daycare worker noticed the child trembling and grimacing. He wouldn't eat and couldn't tell her what was wrong. As she attempted to remove him from the chair, he screamed in pain. She noticed bruises around his abdomen and back. She immediately thought the child had been abused and called his mother, who was on the way. She also called Child Services, whom summoned the sheriff department. Upon arrival at the daycare, the mother was escorted by the sheriff to the hospital. The supervisor for child protective services met them at the hospital as well.

After examination, it was determined that the child had been abused and he was now under the protection and care of child services. It was an event that should have **knocked the mom off balance,** but it was said that she didn't seem surprised. **Wow!** *"Can a mother forget the baby at her breast and have no compassion on the child she has borne? Though she may forget, I will not forget." (Isaiah 49:15).* The next day, the case was turned over to my brother. He would gather information about the little boy, his parents, where was the primary residence, and others who are in the home(s). First, he went to the hospital to check on the little boy. The doctors were examining him more during that time and he was allowed in the room. The child had sustained concussion-like symptoms, broken ribs, burn marks, and there was some scarring around the anal area. The doctors told my brother that the child would be sent to a Children's Hospital 40 miles away for special treatment.

Now, it's time for him to interview the father and everyone in the household during that weekend. First, he'd go to the father's home to begin the interviews. The 20-year old father lived with his mom, dad, and teenage brother. The father stated that the little boy had fallen down a short flight of stairs and must have injured his ribs then. He wasn't sure about the cigarette burns but his dad smoked in the house. The grandmother stated that the child was always around the ash tray where the cigarettes would be burning. The grandfather was usually drunk on the weekends and didn't want to be interviewed. When my brother asked all of them about the suspected anal penetration, the teenage boy started looking at his phone and the grandmother stated that the little boy was constipated when his dad picked him up on Friday. Then, she started blaming the mother for feeding him so much junk food. She said, he was straining to use the bathroom. Trying to keep his cool, my brother could tell that everyone was lying. The father stated that he was in and out of the house all weekend while grandmother and brother helped watch the child.

A couple days later, my brother goes to interview the mother of the child. He notices that she has two other kids- ages 5 and 6. They have a different father than the little boy. Nevertheless, my brother asks her, how well does the little boy get along with the other siblings? She states that they get along well. He asks if they are always in her sight when playing? She says, not always. He continues to ask her about the child's bruises and constipation. She states that the child was fine and playful when they left daycare on Friday. Plus, he had a bowel movement earlier in the week and there didn't appear to be any issues. He also asked her about bathing the child and she said that lately he had been taking baths with his other brothers. **Hmmm... Is she telling the truth or oblivious to what was happening?**

After being on the case for two weeks, my brother said that he had become very stressed and emotional. The little boy was still in the hospital recovering. He had indeed been molested or raped. My brother said that he was getting tired of each parent blaming the other. He started thinking about his current family situation as well. See, he and his wife had recently divorced. They had a one-year old son. The ex-wife is starting to date. Defensively, he instructs her not to bring any men around his little boy. You can imagine, arguments ensued. Crazy, evil thoughts were on his mind. **Can you imagine?** *"On* *this day, thoughts will arise in your mind, and you will devise* *an evil plan." (Ezekiel 38:10).*

Half way through the third week, my brother asked his supervisor to be removed from the case. He cited emotional attachment and feared bad judgement. He would be reprimanded for his actions. He would pray for the little boy's recovery. He'd ask God for forgiveness for his emotions and evil thoughts! Then he would apply and pray for guidance counselor jobs with the school system. Well today, he is a guidance counselor at a local elementary school and he loves his position. Even more, the school appreciates and loves him just as much. Ironically, that abused little boy is now 5 years old and is in kindergarten at the same school. He states that the boy seems to be a good student with good behavior. Also, my brother's little boy attends the school as well in Pre-K. **Isn't God good?**

Teachers

Teachers are enduring more stress than ever before. An article from _npr.org_ in December or 2016 states that *"46% of* *teachers say they feel high daily stress."* I got a chance to see it first-hand. Ironically, it was around this time of the year when a good friend, who is a teacher, said that she doesn't know if she can take it anymore. When I asked her what's wrong, she stated that *"the stress she's enduring from behavior of the students, nonchalant attitudes of fellow teachers, and disappointments of teaching at the current school are not worth it."* She was ready to leave for another school or position.

Not being able to relate to what she was feeling, I didn't know what to tell her other than hang in there because the kids need you. I said, talk to the principal and see what she recommends. She had no confidence and trust in the principal because she had the same attitude as some of the other teachers. So, she had started to **pray** every night and plan her escape. Then, on a Wednesday morning in early December one of her students who could see her stress said to her *"are you going to leave us?"* The student went on to say that *"our teacher from last year was frustrated and she didn't come back after Christmas break."* The student, who had some behavior issues but also a lot of influence on others, said *"you are the only one who seems to care about us and want us to really learn."* He continued to say, *"We're going to do right because we don't want you to leave."* **Wow!** Of course, she tried to hide her emotions from the student, but it made her feel special and re-assured her purpose. All she wanted to do is teach and help the students learn.

Because of that student, she decided to remain at the school at least until the end of the year. Although there were some improvements in her student's behaviors, the school's atmosphere remained challenging the entire year. She continued to **pray** and use some techniques she learned in previous training on dealing with students from dysfunctional families, poverty-stricken households, and communities. The training regimen that she used was very similar to **Ruby K. Payne's** training book on _Understanding and Working with Students and Adults from Poverty and_ Patricia A. Jennings's book titled _Mindfulness for Teachers._

She had her students write a short paragraph on what kind of job they want to have and why. Also, she asked them to write who their role model(s) are and why. The lesson created a lot of interaction and feedback from the entire class. This was not much different than a career day with parents or people in the community, but they were not having any of these days. She would give the students more insight on some of their career choices and role models. She'd also relay to them how these jobs require hard work, drive, determination, critical thinking, maturity, etc. _"Start children off on the way they should go, and even when they are old, they will not turn from it" (Proverbs 22:6)._ These are the same behaviors that you need to put into your lessons every day. She would be able to manage her stress and deal with her classroom challenges and try not to let the chaos outside of class distract her students. It worked.

Knocked Off-Balance

Despite the improvements, she left the school at the end of the year. She continues to work in the educational field. Today, she is a teaching coach who assists middle school teachers with daily activities for their students. Although her stress level has diminished, she is realizing that many of her colleagues-especially the teachers need to go through some of the same training that she has completed. Many of the teachers at the current school are struggling to buy in to her activities and techniques, but she has full support of the Principal. Plus, that's what her job was established for. Dealing with the teacher's attitudes carry a little stress, but she handles it better. She credits her relationship with **God**, her boyfriend, and her children being in a better place, as coping mechanisms. She states that her quality of life outside of work is very good.

Like many other educators, she didn't realize that teaching would be so stressful. Today, the behaviors, attitudes, social media, TV, environment, etc. is making it more challenging for these educators. Yet, many of them get blamed for the demise of the students. The stress in the schools coupled with their own personal life is **knocking teachers off balance and changing their course of life**. Many are seeing their work and life balance in total dysfunction. Because of this reason, many teachers are quitting to pursue other careers.

Teachers, how is your stress level today? What are the causes of your high stress? What are you doing to manage or minimize the stress? How is the work stress affecting your quality of life?

Firefighters

As a little boy, I use to say that I want to be a fireman when I grow up. It was because I was fascinated with the red fire trucks, the sound of the sirens, and the masculine uniforms, hat, and tools they have. Firemen appeared to be real, tough men. Plus, the job looked exciting to see them waving those fire hoses as they sprayed the fires and rescued people from burning buildings. **Can you relate?** What I didn't think about was people dying from explosions, trapped inside and firemen can't get to them, stepping over dead bodies, buildings collapsing, etc. **Wow!** This job seems stressful. It was enough for me as well as others to re-think that career as we got older.

Firemen go through extensive training. They must be in good physical condition with good mental and intestinal fortitude. Their jobs require 24-hour coverage at the stations-often 2-3 consecutive 24- hour coverage. Adequate rest is a must because at any given time, they could be battling fires or rescuing someone for hours. Having a clear head and great teamwork is extremely vital for firemen. You can imagine that with a family, it's tough but clear understanding, good communication, and being grounded helps the relationship.

One of my basketball teammates from college is a fireman in Detroit. He was not looking to become a fireman but the job he worked prior was over-working him and he was often exhausted when off. He stated that he prayed and asked God to find him another job. *"And whatever you ask in prayer, you will receive, if you have faith." (Matthew 21:22).* While speaking to a client one day and mentioning how exhausted he was, the client told him that the fire department was hiring. He told him that they would love to have a tall, physical shaped man like yourself. He also told him about the fireman's training, pay, work schedule, and time off. It sounded good to him. He applied and was hired within weeks. ***"Thank you, God",*** he said.

The training and horrific videos would prepare him for what was to come in real life situations. He told himself that he was ready. Within the first two months on the job, he would respond to over 20 fires, crashes, and rescues. He had gotten burned in one of the fires. Over this span of time, he had witnessed 19 dead bodies. He recalled one response where he tripped and fell over some bodies in an adult daycare fire that took the lives of 12 people. The stress from these events and what potentially lied ahead were over-whelming and had **knocked him off balance.** He started to feel as though he didn't belong in this job. His injuries from the burns gave him time to heal, pray, and plan his course of action.

Then he remembered that he prayed to God for a better job. No one said it would be easy and stress free. He realized the magnitude of the job. He knew that his primarily job duties were helping others, serve, protect, rescue, and fight fires. He asked God, *"am I in the right place?"* He answered the question himself and felt that he was put in the job for a reason. There was no need to stress and doubt his faith in God. Plus, he realized how selfish it would be to give up on rescuing people in need. *"Save others, snatching them out of the fire, and on some have mercy with fear, hating even the garment polluted by the flesh." (Jude 1:23).*

Twenty-five years later, he is still a firefighter. He overcame the challenges in the early months of his career. Although stressful situations still exist, he is better equipped mentally and spiritually to handle them. He takes pride in rescuing people and putting out fires. It's a special feeling having people come up to you thanking you for what you do or what you have done", he said. He goes on to say, *"despite knowing someone may die or that I'm risking my life to save someone, I know that God is with me every step of the way. For that reason, I love my job."*

How is your stress level today on the job? What are you doing about it? Do you feel as though you have the most stressful job in the world? Is the stress affecting your quality of life? Are you developing medical issues due to work stress? Are you praying about it or making changes in your life or a job change? Are you just accepting the way things are a hoping they get better? When work stress occurs, there are many solutions to minimizing or eliminating it. First, one must evaluate what has caused the stress. How could it have been avoided? What are the lessons learned? *"It is good for me that I was afflicted, that I might learn your statutes." (Psalm 119:71).* Of course, quitting the job is not the best option for many of us. On the other hand, we'd like to see or know that our stress can improve with some changes.

All jobs should have goals and objectives, and they must be achievable. Plus, we should be given the right tools to reach those goals. Being humble, dedicated, dependable, feeling appreciated, showing drive and determination helps too! It doesn't hurt to be spiritually equipped as well. *"For we are his workmanship, created in Christ Jesus for good works, which God prepared beforehand, that we should walk in them." (Ephesians 2:10).* We realize that we can't put all our stress in God's hands but knowing he will lend a hand if we ask truly helps.

Chapter 13

Physical Health (Kidney Disease/Diabetes, Cancer, Heart Trouble, Erectile Dysfunction)

Despite hereditary health illnesses, generational poverty, lack of health coverage, and multiple child births, mom was healthy. I never recalled her being very ill. She developed digestive tract issues, high blood pressure, and a touch of diabetes late in her life. Her fear of going to the doctor probably shortened her life because she never thought she was sick. *"Healthy people don't need a doctor, sick people do."* (*Matthew 9:12*). She believed in prayer, old remedies, natural, herbal plants, fruit, leafy vegetables, roots, tea, etc. All these things may have worked but they could only take her so far.

Diabetes and kidney disease ravished by mom's family. **Polycystic Kidney disease**, *an inherited disorder in which clusters of cysts develop in the kidneys*, took the lives of our mother's dad and several of her siblings. Many of her sibling's illnesses went undiagnosed and they didn't live beyond 60 years of age. A couple of them died as infants. A few of their kids were diagnosed with the illness as well. Out of sixteen children, only two of us have been diagnosed with Diabetes and or the kidney disease. Our brother, Elliott, was diagnosed as a juvenile and Rhonda was diagnosed in her late 40's. Elliott did have the kidney disease and went through dialysis for 10 years before succumbing to the illness at the age of 47. Because the disease is hereditary, all of us are watching our diet and getting our kidneys and blood sugar checked during doctor's visits.

We recently connected with some of our first cousins on mom's side of the family. One of her brothers, who died from the illness, had nine kids. One of his daughters was diagnosed with the kidney disease as a teenager. She would get sick often, but her siblings thought that she was just trying to get attention. She would be placed on a couple different medications-one for her kidney functions and one for control of high blood pressure. None of her other siblings had the disease and she would often ask God, *"Why me?"* when she'd feel ill.

By age nineteen, the illness is controlled but not going away. She starts a relationship and gets pregnant. Her little girl is born with the kidney disease. In fact, the child's kidneys are so enlarged, that she looks deformed and or malnourished. Atop of that, the doctors inform her that the little girl would be lucky to make it past the age of five. **Can you say knocked off balance!** My cousin knew that the risks were high, but she was willing to take that chance even though the consequences could be life altering. At that time, she believed in the power of prayer and didn't fret the doctor's prognosis. *"for he had healed many, with the result that all those who had afflictions pressed around Him, in order to touch Him." (Mark 3:10).* The care for the child would change her course of life. Under the supervision of the doctors, prayer, and family support, she would ensure her child got what she needed.

Her daughter's condition was progressing, but her boyfriend couldn't handle the situation. Before you knew it, she is caring for her child alone. Her sisters would offer her as much support as they could, but they had families too. A few years later, she meets her husband. He seemed to be a loving and caring man. He accepted her daughter as though she was his own. A year later, she gets pregnant and has a little boy. Initial prognosis is good but there's a trace of cysts in his kidneys but nothing to worry about. She starts to feel as though life is getting somewhat normal, but husband seems as though he's becoming stressed out. The marriage has begun to get a little rocky. She's already fragile yet the husband has become abusive. They would separate a short time later.

Over the next few years, she would endure a series of unexpected events. Her mom passed away in the early 1990's. At age 29, she became very ill and in need of a kidney. One of her sisters was a perfect match and would give one of her kidneys. Unfortunately, her body rejected the kidney a short time later. She would go on to be totally dependent on dialysis. Her dad, who helped care for her kids while she recovered from the failed transplant and start of dialysis, passed away from complications from Diabetes in 1994. In early 1997, her daughter, now a senior in high school, became very ill. This time both kidneys had failed completely and had to be removed. **Wow! Can you say knocked off balance!** Keep in mind that she wasn't predicted to be here at age 17.

There was one bright spot during that timeframe and that was my cousin and her husband at reconciled. Her daughter would start dialysis and graduate from high school. She would work some at the local grocery store and Walmart for a few years. She would be on the donor's list for years, but my cousin was fretting her body rejecting them just as she did. She would envision a lot of suffering for her daughter. She would continue dialysis for nearly fifteen years before succumbing to the illness at the age of 31. *"Trust in the Lord with all your heart, and do not lean on your own understanding." (Proverbs 3:5).* It became difficult for my cousin to trust doctors and have faith in God. She would ask, "if you are one who can heal, then why take her away." Shortly after her daughter's death, her son's kidneys started to fail, and he begins dialysis as well. Now, they both begin to question

God's existence. Although she wishes no ill will on anyone, she still asks "why is she and her kids cursed?"

Recently, her son received a new kidney and it's functioning well. She had another kidney transplant that failed as well. Today, she has no kidneys and continues dialysis three times a week. She doesn't fear death and continues to live the best life that she can. She is writing short stories which have recently been published. She's a certified health coach and a ESRD consultant for those facing difficult choices about kidney failure. She has also started her own business called **Raintree Nutrition Works** which teaches natural ways to treat health issues.

One of my brothers and his ex-wife had a son late in life. It was his first son and he was so excited. He would envision taking him fishing and participating in sports which is some of his top hobbies. The little boy is adorable and a spitting image of his dad. Many family members would offer to babysit him while his dad would referee youth basketball. At the age of two, the little boy wanted to attend some of the games with his dad. So, my brother would bring along a nephew or niece to watch over him at the gym. In between games, his son would run out on the court wanting the ball. He was crazy about basketball. My brother is thrilled and awaiting to teach him the game along with other things.

Over the next six months, his little boy would get sick often. It went from catching a cold to contagious viruses at daycare. Then rashes would form around his hands and feet. Two different doctors diagnosed him with **hand, foot, and mouth disease.** It's a common children's virus causing sores in the mouth and rashes on the hands and feet. The doctors told my brother and his ex-wife not to worry that it would go away within a few weeks if treated right. Well, the virus kept coming and going. They were blaming the spread of the virus on the daycare. Upon being examined by a nephrologist, their little boy was diagnosed with **juvenile diabetes. Can you say knocked off balance!**

Both were devastated with the news. Satan would show his face momentarily as the ex-wife would state that the disease is a curse from our family heritage although diabetes history is on both sides of the child's family. My brother would complain about how adamant she was to put their son in that specific daycare. The daycare was full of kids from military families who may have brought some diseases from overseas and that was the contributing force. **Wow! Satan will come and bring distractions when times are tough causing you to lose focus of the task at hand.** Each one of them were facing a change in their course of life. Prayer and guidance is needed. Discipline would be highly required. They realized that it would be challenging but it could be done.

The son had to be placed on a strict diet with little to no sugar and low carbs. His love for applesauce, cheerios, candy, etc. had to be sugar-free and monitored. He would have insulin pods attached to his body to inject insulin when his blood sugar levels are out of balance. He would have his little finger pricked daily to verify his blood sugar. His care is now requiring constant monitoring with instructions. My brother and his ex-wife can no longer have just anyone babysitting for them. It was very difficult for the child to understand what was going on, but he understood certain things would make him sick.

Today, it has been nearly two years since the diagnosis and the child has adapted to the diet. Although there remains a long road ahead, they all have overcome the initial challenges. Their little boy is now in Pre-K and is doing well. Fortunately, he attends the same school where his daddy is working, and he's monitored regularly.

Cancer

"A disease in which abnormal cells divide uncontrollably and destroy body tissue." (American Cancer Society). Cancer does not discriminate. It affects all nationalities, children, men, women, animals, etc. Of course, undiagnosed, late treatment, or untreated will result in death.

We all know the affects. When discovered, it knocks you and loved ones off balance. Often, the diagnosis changes your course of life. Treatment requires strength, courage, strong will, discipline amongst medical treatment such as chemotherapy. It doesn't hurt to add **prayer** too.

My grandmother died from an unknown cancer in her 50's. Mom passed away from complications associated with gangrenous of the small intestines-which could have possibly been a form of cancer. My dad passed away from **prostate cancer**. One of our brothers passed away from a form of **esophageal cancer**. As you see, cancer runs deep in our family history. Periodic medical check-ups should be incorporated in all our lives. Of course, there are some forms of cancer that are induced by our bad habits such as: smoking, drugs, alcohol, diet, untreated illnesses and infections, etc. Can you relate?

One of my great nephews was diagnosed with **Stage IVB Hodgkin Lymphoma** at the age of 9. The news caught the entire family by storm. His mother and father were **temporarily knocked off balance**. They realized that their lives would be altered. The child was going to need them to be strong and encouraging. They would have to pull their emotions together and listen to the instructions of the physicians. The physicians would inform them that the cancer is treatable and curable but will require chemo-therapy and radiation. They both agreed to the treatment.

Their lives had completely changed. Both would go on FMLA for a couple months. Eventually, my niece would have to quit work due to the constant care and doctor's appointments. It was taking a toll on them financially and emotionally. There was a lot of stress in the marriage. Prior to this unexpected event, they were not **grounded** and had not incorporated **God** in their lives. That changed quickly. They realized that all needed prayer and encouragement. *"Therefore encourage one another and build one another up, just as you are doing."* *(Thessalonians 5:11)*. Not only for their son, but for their financial and relationship status. They both admit that it was extremely challenging but with consistent care, teamwork, family support, encouragement, prayer, and the grace of God, they persevered.

With the assistance from the Make a Wish Foundation and the Ronald McDonald House, their son gained strength and courage to fight hard for his life. Those two organizations brought fun, excitement, and courage to them all. Their son got a chance to meet his favorite entertainer (Beyoncé) and his spirit rose to the top. After a long year of strict diets, chemo, and radiation, his lymphoma went into remission. Today, he is a college student and cancer free. Although many of you may have different beliefs but in this case, my niece and her husband praised **God**.

Two years ago, one of my nieces was diagnosed with
Stage IIIB Breast Cancer. The doctors informed her that it was
an aggressive cancer and primarily in her left breast. He stated
that she will need immediate treatment before it spreads.
Knocked off balance, she would need a little time to gather her
emotions. Her husband was right there at her side supporting
her 100%. The next day without conferring with her husband,
she was fearing the treatment and thinking of with-going the
treatment and put it in God's hand. When she informed her
husband of her thoughts, he told her that *"God is an awesome
God, but he wants you to open up your heart and soul to fight
and he will guide you. He can't do it by himself, but he'll be by
your side and so will I"*. **Wow!** That's love and support. *"Fear
not, I am with you; be not dismayed, for I am God; I will
strengthen you, I will help you, I will uphold you with my
righteous right hand." (Isiah 41:10)*.

With that said, my niece received great support and
encouragement from her husband, family, and friends. She
began her treatment a week later. The treatment would start
with the removal of as many as 22 cancerous lymph nodes from
her left breast. Chemo-therapy and radiation would begin
immediately thereafter. The chemo would continue well over a

year. Her husband would remain at her side throughout the entire ordeal. He would encourage her to live, keep your head up, stay upbeat and in good spirits. They would pray together and keep asking God for strength and healing. My niece and her husband had incorporated Jesus Christ in their lives years ago. His years in the military taught him the importance of having faith in God. As you see, they were a little more **grounded**. I believe that does make a difference. Today, her cancer is not in remission yet, but she no longer needs chemo-therapy. She is back to doing her job as an educational specialist with challenged kids. She goes to her radiologist regularly for follow-ups. She tries to eat healthy daily and incorporates exercise. She's carrying on with her life and continues to strive towards her purpose. Above all, she says that *"she's blessed to have a wonderful husband who praises **God** just as much as she does."*

Heart Trouble

As far as I know, there is no history of heart disease or any other type of heart trouble in our family. Now, without a doubt, there's been a lot of broken hearts. That's very damaging to your physical health too. **Do you know what I mean?** *"Keep your heart with all vigilance, for from it flow the springs of life." (Proverbs 4:23)*. Throughout my life, I have been blessed to have good health. As a child, I recall the doctor telling my mom that I had a **heart murmur** during a routine examination. He said it was nothing to be alarmed about but wanted to inform us in case something is discovered later in life. I was very active in sports most of my childhood and adult life. Running, jumping, playing all kinds of sports with no signs of fatigue related to the heart. Later, while in college, I struggled with my lung function while trying to hold my breath for swim class and running a timed mile during basketball training. Although, that was not a heart function, I was diagnosed with asthma.

We all realize that heart conditions do not have to be hereditary. Poor diet, lack of exercise, alcohol, drugs, stress, etc. are all contributing factors to poor heart functionality. In the spring of 2014, I felt some tightness in my chest and shortness of breath. It was early in the morning and the only thing I had eaten that morning was a banana. I went to the company nurse at work and told her my symptoms and asked if she could take my blood pressure. My blood pressure was high, and she recommended that I leave a go to the ER due to the symptoms I was having. After an EKG and examination, it was determined that my heart was fine, but I had indigestion coupled with an asthma flare up. **Whew!** What I sigh of relief. The doctor informed me that I need to eat healthier and stop eating so late at night. He also wrote me a prescription for indigestion and my asthma symptoms.

One year later, while refereeing youth basketball, I felt my heart racing. I thought that maybe I was tired because I had already completed 6 games. I informed my refereeing partner that I needed to sit out a game. Well, my heart didn't stop racing and I proceeded to referee 3 more games anyway. I know you're saying, wow, that's dangerous. But, I felt fine other than the racing heart. This was on a Saturday afternoon. On Monday, my heart wasn't racing as much but it was out of rhythm. That morning, I went to a convenient care center. Another EKG was administered and this time, I am diagnosed with **Atrial Fibrillation.** The doctor informed me that I was not in any immediate danger, but my heart is not going to get back in rhythm on its own. Plus, the current condition could cause a stroke due to potential clotting. When I asked, "how do I get it back in rhythm, he said we'll have to schedule a cardio-version to have it shocked back in rhythm. **Can you say knocked off balance!**

Upon being educated on A-Fib, I found out that it was very common. Many people including professional athletes have been diagnosed with the condition. So, I gathered myself and prepared for the procedure. To hear possible stroke and shocking your heart back in rhythm sounded scary. **Can you relate!** I would be place on a prescription drug Eliquis for 30 days to prepare for the procedure. I would pray often during that 30 days. One of my brothers and my girlfriend would accompany me to the hospital for the procedure. Setting up for the procedure and anesthesia took a couple hours. The procedure itself only took about 10 minutes. When I awakened, the doctors informed me that everything went well. They would monitor me for another hour then I was free to go home. I'm told that I should be able to resume normal activities within a few days.

A week later, I had a follow up to ensure my heart was still in rhythm and it was. I asked the doctor what may have triggered this condition. He said that it's difficult to pinpoint the exact causes due to everyone usually having different contributing factors. I informed him of my issues which included stress, lack of rest, poor diet, enhancement supplements for erectile dysfunction, anxiety, and excitement about moving back to Nashville. All could have played a part, but he can't confirm that. Nevertheless, I would remain on Eliquis for another thirty days then take a coated aspirin once a day. Well, I would move back to Nashville, Tennessee a month later to help my youngest son as he battled **Depression.** He was ecstatic to have me back and he moved in with me immediately. He is now a senior in high school and everything is going well. Months have passed, and I have begun to date multiple women again. I am experimenting with different supplements to enhance my erectile dysfunction. Just after the 4th of July in 2016, my heart was out of rhythm again. **Wow!** I would need the same procedure again or a cardiac ablation-procedure which guides a tube through a pulmonary vein to the heart. The ablation is an invasive option which is very successful. Not wanting any of my veins tampered with, I elected to have the cardio-version again.

At this point, I realized that I must change my ways. Multiple dating must cease. A healthier diet is much needed. I must incorporate more exercise. I want to live without major heart conditions. As I look back on the contributing factors, I feel confident that the enhancements triggered my A-Fib. Many of the supplements and or enhancement pills state "if you have heart conditions, that you may not want to take this pill." The doctors told me that may not have been the factor because I didn't have heart trouble prior to the pills. Ironically, I had taken **vardenafil inhibitor pills** around the time of each episode. **Hmmmm...** I know it wasn't stress the second time because it was very low. Nevertheless, my life was still out of balance. The pills worked but there were consequences that came along with them. I could be wrong, but I don't want to take that chance again. I will deal with my bouts with erectile dysfunction differently.

Erectile Dysfunction

"One in four men under age of 40 may experience some form of Erectile Dysfunction." (The Journal of Sexual Medicine, June 2013). Erectile Dysfunction is a touchy and embarrassing thing that many of us men reframe from discussing with friends and family. Many of those members who are not grounded and or can't relate often smirk or judge. I sought a lot of medical and psychological help for my condition. Plus, I spent a lot of money doing so. Whether it was impatience, inconsistency with the treatment, or continued frustration, I was not getting the results that I wanted.

The Mayo Clinic states that *"male sexual arousal is a complex process that involves the brain, hormones, emotions, nerves, muscles and blood vessels. Erectile dysfunction can result from a problem with any of these. Likewise, **stress and mental health** concerns can cause or worsen erectile dysfunction."* Furthermore, the clinic mentioned some of the physical causes of erectile dysfunction as well. Here are some of those causes: *heart disease, clogged blood vessels, diabetes, **sleep disorders, high cholesterol**, high blood pressure, **enlarged prostate**, metabolic syndrome-which includes high blood* *pressure, high insulin levels, and **body fat around the stomach area,** and surgeries or **injuries around the pelvic area.*** Of course, **genetics**, **diet**, tobacco use, drugs, **alcohol**, and **lack of rest** are contributing factors too. **Oh Wow!** Ironically, all these conditions in bold exist or have existed in my life.

I realized that I had and or still have a lot of the symptoms that could contribute to my erectile dysfunction. Most were items unmentioned during medical or psychological examination and maybe the result was the wrong treatment. Either way, I had an **imbalance** for a large part of my adult life. There was constant **anxiety**, poor diet with a lot of processed foods, enlarged prostate, and an injury in the pelvic area multiple times as a teenager. **Hmmm.....** As I reached adulthood, got marriage, and entered the work environment, other life events occurred that didn't improve my situation. There was stress and more anxiety, inconsistent exercise, and inadequate rest and relaxation. I was doing too much and neglecting my own physical and mental well-being. Plus, I was not incorporating God in my life. I was looking for a quick fix and resolution to my condition but not seeking the right guidance.

As I began to make more changes in my personal life, I

realized that I also need to include some spiritual growth. I read *John 5:1-17* which talked about the *"healing of the impotent man at Bethesda"* and that bible's chapter made me want to try something different. That man had been sick for 38 years and was afraid to step into the pool of water that an angel had purposely trouble for Jesus healing of the sick, crippled, troubled, and blind. **Why was he so afraid?** My conclusion is like many of us today. We don't know Jesus and what he is capable of. So, we say, *"I've been this way for years. How am I going to trust someone that I don't know? What's the point?"* **Can you relate?**

A year ago, I had begun to do some self-reflecting. It was time to give up the old life and step into the new. I was not going to bring old things into this new life. I begin to date only one woman whom is wonderful. I am intending church more for which I'm now incorporating the lessons learned in my daily life. I am eating healthier, exercising, and using natural remedies for my ED. Primarily, those remedies entail low stress and anxiety, proper rest, relaxation and fun with my girlfriend, no pressure, great conversation, and spiritual growth. Ironically, the more consistent I am with this regiment, my erectile dysfunction is greatly improved. Of course, this may not be everyone's solution. What about you?

Many of us have similar and or different physical

limitations. All may require different treatment. Oftentimes, we need time to think about it and or get a second opinion. We may need to build up courage and strength. Encouragement, love, and support from our loved ones is much needed. Ironically, many of us who didn't believe in **God** or thought we'd never need him began to pray. He's always there whether you ask for him or not. We all should strive to take care of our bodies. Let us not be tempted to indulge in things that we know will cause us health issues! Don't you desire to have a clean bill of health? Know your family medical history! There's a reason that we're asked before a doctor's examination. At any given point in our lives, we will face some type of medical condition. It may knock us off balance. If it's not a condition that calls for immediate care, get fully educated about it. Ensure you are making the right decision and getting the right treatment! Pray for healing and ask God for guidance! *"For he wounds, but he binds up; he shatters, but his hands heal." (Job 5:18).*

Chapter 14

Mental Health (Anxiety, Depression, and PTSD)

Mental Health can be summarized as a mental imbalance that affects one's emotions, psychological, and social well-being. The conditions affect how you would think, feel, and act. It also determines how you handle stress, relate to others, and make decisions. *MentalHealth.gov.* These conditions affect many of us and our loved ones. Oftentimes, the illnesses go undiagnosed, they're looked over as behavior issues, or we're in denial. When diagnosed or a tragic event occurs because of someone's mental state, it could **knock you off balance and change your course of life.**

Today, it appears to be many more mentally ill people in our society. Is it the stress, anxiety, pressures, fears, beliefs, drugs, alcohol, traumatic experiences, the environment, or genetics? Whatever reasons, many of us struggle to cope with life. Some of us become judgmental, form our own opinions, or briefly discuss it. Then the conditions occur in you, your loved ones, or someone in your circle. Wow! You never imagined it would hit home, right. Now, how do you handle it?

As I look back on my mom's journey, it's unbelievable that she never fell apart. Anxiety and Depression was lurking around the entire family. There was daily anxiety. Although she and her kids were left uncovered by her husband, she didn't walk alone. She believed that God didn't intend for her to just give up and become an emotional wreck. *"The Lord himself goes before you and will be with you; he will never leave you nor forsake you. Do not be afraid; do not be discouraged."* (<u>*Deuteronomy 31:8*</u>). My mom read her bible and prayed every night and I believe she had this scripture in her mind throughout her life.

As we got older, mom realized that it would be impossible to save us all from the lure of anxiety and depression. But, she tried anyway. She could see it on our faces, in our attitudes, demeanor, and the way we talked. She would encourage us to pray but most of us didn't have that spirit or walk with the Lord. She'd tell us to *"not get caught up in the devil's trap. If there's a will, there's a way."* At times, some of us would become over-whelmed and didn't know what to do or who to turn to. Although mom was a "superwoman", she could not shield us all.

There are some serious mental disturbances in our society such as paranoia, schizophrenia, psychosis, bipolar disorders, and others. Oftentimes, many of us don't associate anxiety, depression, and PTSD as serious disturbances but they all can lead to some serious problems including suicide.

Anxiety

According to Medical News Today, *anxiety is a general term for several disorders that cause nervousness, fear, apprehension, and worrying. The disorders could affect how we feel and behave. Furthermore, they could manifest into real, physical symptoms. Is it a mental disturbance or natural reaction?*

Without question, mom and most of her children suffered from anxiety. Even when Mr. Scott was home, there were worries about food, clothing, and shelter. Because he didn't hold a steady job, there was a lot of instability. The foundation was always shaky. When he left for good, mom's anxiety went to another level. Fear set in. There were moments of depression too, but she persevered.

As youths, I think all of us had moments of shame and embarrassment. There were many times that my siblings skipped school because they worried about how they looked (mainly clothing and shoes). While in school, some of my siblings stated that they were very apprehensive when the teachers asked them to come and write something on the board. Although many of the students didn't tease them personally, there was snickering when they approached or walked by. Can you imagine or relate?

My Battle with Anxiety

As a teenager in high school, that's when my anxiety surfaced. I'd worry about not having money to buy certain clothes, shoes, and sports gear. Going into the 10th grade, I had a bicycle accident that resulted in a broken right wrist. Now in a cast, I couldn't write very fast and I was getting behind on my work. I was an honor roll student and now I worried about my grades slipping. Peer pressure was brewing too. The weekend parties have now included slow dancing music, marijuana, alcohol, and potential after party sex. I never got persuaded with drugs or alcohol but my desire for sex was different. All my male friends were sexually active-so they said.

On another note, I'm excited yet nervous about being the starting point guard for the varsity basketball team. I had just recovered from the broken wrist. Plus, all my friends are on the JV team. **Can you see things potentially getting out of balance?** There's a whole lot going on at one time. This doesn't seem much different than many but keep in mind that everyone's mental framework if different. Furthermore, my family structure is not **grounded**.

Later that year, I had one young lady who was pursuing me heavily. At first, I was a little timid and shy but she was energetic, outgoing, and made me laugh. She was not in the pretty girl click nor was she in the gifted and talented. I was a smart jock and several of my female friends thought that I should be dating a cheerleader. Well, we like who we like, right. Plus, she was already sexually active. **Hmmm...** We began to date and started a relationship. During conversations, she'd inform me that she had been sexually active since early 9th grade. Thinking with the wrong head, I became **anxious** of course. Not sure of how it would go down when the opportunity to engage in sexual intercourse presented itself, I began to feel a little **nervous**. Can you relate? She was an aggressive young lady. As our grandmothers would say, she was "**hot in the ass**." That made me even more nervous to which I'm worried about my performance on my first sexual encounter. I knew I wasn't mentally ready, but I was excited and impatient. *"Patience is the key, because, when the right time comes, it will be very beautiful and totally worth the wait." (LiveLiveHappy.com).*

Well, it happened, and it wasn't beautiful. My confidence was shattered. I was **knocked off balance**. I was embarrassed and felt less than a man. Although my girlfriend told me not to worry about it, I was disappointed. I wasn't ready, but I wanted something to boast and brag about to my friends. **Wow!** Now, if exposed, I could be the **laughing stock** of my circle. Imagine that! My father was not around to tell me about the *birds and the bees*. I didn't know who to confide in without feeling embarrassed.

Although mom was playing the role of mother and father, I didn't feel comfortable talking to her about sex. We didn't have that spiritual background to teach me that it's ok to wait-preferably until marriage. In fact, in my community or socio-economic group, I vaguely recall anyone mention *wait till marriage*. Furthermore, it was never mentioned in my household or my circle of friends. I believe mom felt like a hypocrite to tell any of us to wait. Eventually, my nerves improved and so did my performance.

Take a moment to think about your first sexual encounter! Were you confident, scared, or nervous? How did it turn out for you? Were you left craving the next encounter or disappointed in the outcome? Did you feel pressured to get it over with? I realize that I am being very transparent with my words, but these words are all, in an effort, to help others. Think about the effects from anxiousness and or pressured sexual encounters! For many, it may have gone well. For those who had a bad experience, what was the impact? How has it affected your life or someone in your circle today?

Looking back at that moment, I believe that initial encounter affected my confidence in other parts of my life. I realized that I had put too much pressure on myself to perform. Not only sexually but in other aspects of my life. When all I needed to do was exhibit patience, trust the process, and let it come naturally. I was running a race and I needed to get to the finish line quickly. I feared being last and potentially teased or ridiculed. *"Let there be no filthiness nor foolish talk nor crude joking, which are out of place, but instead let there be thanksgiving." (Ephesians 5:4).*

In some socio-economic groups, why is it such a big deal to lose your virginity at such a young age-especially the young men? That first time should be special to all or should it. No stress and no pressure! Preferably, we should be in a relationship leading to marriage. Today, it's hard for young adults to remain abstinent. Not only is sex on the brain, but it's everywhere-commercials, billboards, social media, television shows, and schools. If your teenagers are reframing from sex, we applaud your parenting, the church if that's part of it, and groundwork.

Prior to starting my college basketball career, my

friends and family were confident that my ability, if I remain healthy, would take me to the next level. Well, I injured my right ankle at the beginning of my freshman year and it required surgery. I missed the entire season. I worried about my lateral, horizontal, and vertical movement following recovery. With good therapy, weight training, diet, and other training, I came back the next year in the best shape of my life-mentally and physically. I was ready to play.

When the season rolled around, the coaches were impressed with my game and my physical growth. My teammates thought that I was one of the **top practice players** in the country. No one wanted to guard me. I was very quick with good ball-handling skills. Plus, I had a near picture-perfect jump shot with some serious hang-time. Wow! That was an awesome feeling. When team press day came, I was named a starter at shooting guard. Feeling very anxious, I would have **butterflies in my stomach** prior to the game (form of nervousness). It was a common thing-not just for me but other players as well. Some players would be jittery, sweating profusely, need to take a crap, and or throw up before the game. Oftentimes, we'd need that first shot, steal, dunk, block, or free throw to calm the nerves. Can you relate?

I struggled to get past the nerves. Ten games into the season, my practice play had not carried over into the live games. I was averaging seven points, shooting 30% from the field, and four turn-overs per game. Those were terrible stats for a shooting guard. I began to put unnecessary pressure on myself due to my mistakes. I was not taking the coaches constructive criticism well and I was displeased with my game. I was apprehensive with my decision making on the court and feared being benched because of the wrong decisions. My anxiety had taken over. I lacked the confidence to push myself. I was starting to collapse mentally. Before you knew it, the coach had lost confidence in me and I was benched and played sparingly the remainder of the season.

I needed help in multiple ways but didn't realize it and apparently, neither did others at that time. The coaches and fellow players thought I just didn't have **"Heart"** or intestinal fortitude. In these masculine sports, if you seem to falter due to instability, you're labeled as *"soft or weak."* The coaching staff had no confidence in me but they didn't give up. They hoped that I would pull it together. The next year, my anxiety was about the same. I became nervous when called upon. I worried more about making mistakes than making things happen.

I had all the raw ability that a player could ask for, but I lacked the confidence and strength to overcome my anxiety. Because of that, my basketball career was in the tank. I could have used some psychological counseling and prayer. Although we said the "Lord's Prayer" before every game as a team, I never thought to pray individually for strength and courage to overcome the nervousness, apprehensions, and worries. *"Do not be anxious about anything, but in everything by prayer and supplication with thanksgiving, let your requests be known to God." (Philippians 4:6).* Although mom had given me a small bible, I didn't know that I needed that kind of help. Therefore, I didn't know what to ask for. Individual prayer was the farthest thing from my mind. Is your student-athlete exhibiting these behaviors? If so, don't wait to intervene.

Going into my junior year, my oldest son was born. Suddenly, my anxiety began to grow even more. I needed a job to help support my son. The coach that brought me in had gotten fired. We have a totally new coaching staff. They brought in several new players. The head coach was meeting with some of the old and new players prior to conditioning. I was missing in action because I was working. When the head coach finally met me, he didn't think I was serious about playing because I missed pre-season meetings and scrimmages. Although it shouldn't have mattered, he didn't know that I had a child at the time. Yet, I was reluctant to tell him.

Prior to the start of the season, I was dismissed from the team. The athletic department and team members informed the coach that he is making a mistake by releasing Clayvon. So, instead of bringing me back to the team, he forced me to try out with other potential walk-ons at 5am in the morning. **Wow!** Well, I wasn't a quitter and not only did I show up, I was head and shoulders above all potential players that morning. Even the assistant coaches were wondering why I was dismissed in the first place. I was brought back but heavily criticized by the head coach. I took a knee to the thigh a day before the first scrimmage and it caused severe pain and a deep bruise. It hampered my mobility. I was unable to play in the scrimmage. The coach took it as **"being soft"** and I was dismissed again for good! **Can you say knocked off balance!**

I wasn't sure what I was going to do without basketball. A little fear had set in, but I still had my scholarship-at least till the end of the year. I worried about what my friends and family would think when I tell them. I had become a waste of talent and felt embarrassed. I contemplated on transferring to other schools to continue playing but I felt as though my heart and love for the game was ripped away. I needed help, counseling, and support from someone who could relate. My girlfriend and mother of my child was there for me but she couldn't relate or help me through this ordeal. So, I just blamed myself and distanced myself from the team.

The team struggled severely under the new coach. Several of the new players had no impact on the team. One was dismissed for drugs, another flunked out of school, and the coach was fired within three years. In later years, several teammates told me how my dismissal affected the team-especially when they saw the struggles from players whom the coach thought would replace me. They wondered how it would have been to have me playing.

It's amazing how events or stages of your life changes one's mental framework. During my middle school through 10th grade years, I was fearless and hardly ever nervous about anything. Although poor, I had little worries about necessities. I was very smart, well-liked, good mannerisms, and the teacher's pet in school. I looked forward to standing up in front of class and reciting Shakespeare. Every sport that I played, I was well above average. Many who knew me, would say I was extremely gifted. In basketball, as *Stewart Scott* from ESPN would say, *"he's smooth like silk and as cool as the other side of the pillow"*. Well, that may not have been any different than many other athletes at that age. Of course, real life begins in the early adolescent years and you must be prepared and ready to tackle it head on. Although I had the gifts, I was not fully **equipped**.

My basketball career had ended, but life had to go on. I had to take a year off because there was no more scholarship money. Upon establishing in state tuition status, I re-entered school and graduated in May of 1992. Four months later, I married my child's mother. A month later, I landed a good job with good pay and benefits. It was a blessing. The job had nothing to do with my BBA degree, but it increased my salary from an entry level retail job by 50%. Plus, the opportunity for advancement was imminent. With that job, I became very versatile and received several promotions, awards, and certificates. It has given me an opportunity to travel abroad to Canada and Japan. Twenty-five years later, I am still employed with the same company.

Today, although I still love the game, I have no regrets from my failure of basketball. It has helped me grow into the man I am today. I learned that my gifts and talents are very broad and extend well beyond the game of basketball. Believe it or not, I still possess those same qualities that I had in middle school. Well, I may be a step or two slower on the court or field but don't be mistaken. Although I have struggled with anxiety throughout my life, I have found some resolve. Rest and Relaxation are at the top of the list. Enjoying time with my young men and other family members are high as well! Being transparent, listening actively, and understanding has helped me grow into a good relationship with my girlfriend which is leading to that ultimate goal. Above all, I have incorporated **Jesus Christ** and I'm at peace with my life. There's a sermon I love by _T.D Jakes_ titled, _"God promotes you on your heart not your talents."_. I am discovering this spirit every day.

Physical Effects from Anxiety/Stress

According to _WebMD_, there are many physical effects associated with anxiety and stress. The reactions are different for each individual person. Some may experience headaches, nausea, weakness, or dizziness. Other symptoms may include chest pains, tense muscles, colds and cold sores, infections, break outs(rashes), insomnia, and low energy.

Around the age of 14, my middle son would break out with rashes on his face. During that time, he was a catcher for his baseball team. Initially, we thought that it was due to sweat, heat, and constant rubbing from the facemask. We treated it with anti-bacteria soap and soothing ointment. It would go away for a little while but come back within a week. We took him to his pediatrician who recommended a dermatologist. The dermatologist diagnosed his rash as a bacterial infection. He prescribed a steroid cream for treatment. The cream worked, somewhat. The rashes would still come and go.

Upon follow up visits, the dermatologist would say that applying the cream while his face was moist was not allowing the medicine to work. He reiterated to us that our son needs to apply the cream an hour or so after washing his face or showering and to ensure his face was dry. Maybe a couple hours prior to going to bed. Also, apply when there's no physical activities. We did just what the doctor said but the rashes would continue to come and go. Seven years later, my son continues to have occasional break outs. **Hmmm....**

In the spring of 2016, now a sophomore in college, he

had the worst break out of all. He was embarrassed to go to class. Upon going to the college infirmary, the nurse told him that it may be **Lupus**-*an inflammatory disease caused when the immune system attacks its own tissues.* After reading about the disease and discovering it was incurable and deadly, he became distraught. **Can you say knocked off balance!** To calm his worries, I informed him that I seriously doubt that's what you have. I told him that we would schedule a physical examination with blood work. The examination and blood work revealed no signs of Lupus.

It didn't dawn on me until recently that maybe he needed to see a different doctor. When he told me about his school workload, group presentation assignments, and trying to work a job, I realized that my son was anxious and stressed. He was suffering from stress and anxiety. When he gets nervous or anxious, the reaction from his body caused rashes on his face. **Wow! Can you relate?** For many of us, stress and anxiety appear in different forms for different individuals. His facial flare-ups during his baseball playing days were not from sweat and or dirty facemask. It was nervousness, pressure, apprehension, and stress. When the flare-ups occurred, the sweat and dirty facemask kept the rashes from healing quicker. The doctors that he had seen were not psychiatrists, so they were not going to ask questions about his mental well-being because there wasn't a problem that we knew of.

Today, he hasn't seen a therapist yet, but we are scheduling an appointment as this book is being written. Now, stress and anxiety may not be the full underlying issue for his break outs, but it's definitely related. In the meantime, he finds ways to relax, rest, and ease in mind. His flare-ups are little to none when the stress is low. He puts first things first which is his education. He prays every day and asks God for strength, guidance, and calmness. He channels his stress and anxiety into helping young athletes achieve success through sports ministry. He feels that using a sports platform, especially baseball, is helping him discover his purpose. *"You make known to me the path of life; in your presence there is fullness of joy; at your right hand are pleasures forevermore." (Psalm 16:11).*

How is anxiety affecting your life today? Do you feel as though it doesn't exist in your life? How are you overcoming it? Do you realize that left untreated, without counseling, medicines, or God, could lead to other mental imbalances?

Chronic Depression

As teenagers, many of us thought we were grown(adults) when we reached the adolescent years. No one could tell us what to do and or how to do it. We already knew the answers. We weren't worried about our homework. We didn't fret about inadequate rest. We stated that we wouldn't subject ourselves to the mischief and behaviors of our friends. We would procrastinate with many activities. Can you recall those moments! Unfortunately, we had to learn the hard way. Then, it was an *"I told you so moment."* Now, your *"know it all attitude"* has caused poor judgement and has incurred some serious consequences. For a moment, you may experience some chronic depression.

Although undiagnosed, I believe my oldest son is struggling with that now. Of course, he doesn't think so. He is physically fit with no current health issues. He umpires baseball from March through October and works a regular job. Although he says that he's ok with his life, he remains hung up on past disappointments. He is doing ok but lacks drive and motivation to move forward and on his own. He has some insomnia. He doesn't care to do some things that were once a big part of his life. He fears stepping out of his comfort zone. He's very judgmental at times and he stereo-types other people. He is slightly out of touch with real life. Maybe, it's because he hasn't been fully equipped. I am trying to get him to understand that **his thoughts and or perceptions are not reality**. Do you know someone who thinks like this too? *"The natural person does not accept the things of the Spirit of God, for they are folly to him, and he is not able to understand them because they are* *spiritually discerned." (1 Corinthians 2:14).*

Here's his story!

He aspired to be a college baseball player but team personnel issues during his high school years forced him out of his comfort zone. He was a really good centerfielder and starter as a freshman. At the end of the season, he was feeling good about himself, the team, and school. He was on the watch list for Nashville high school's up and coming baseball players. The coach praised him for being a solid player and looked forward to coaching him for the remainder of his high school baseball career.

The following year, there were several changes with the team. The coach moved my son from centerfield to left field because a player returned from missing the previous season. My son adapted to the change with no problem. Then, midway through the season, several players were dismissed from the team due to poor conduct. Following the dismissals, the coach made my son the catcher. He hadn't played this position in five years and he was totally out of his comfort zone. It affected his entire game. His attitude was different and disappointment was on his face often. He couldn't wait for the season to end.

Feeling as though he needed a lift from a disappointing sophomore year of baseball, his friends convinced him to play football his junior year. It didn't seem to be a bad thing, but he hadn't played since 8th grade. At season start, he was named a starter at cornerback. He was super excited and was off to a good start. The team finished the regular season 9-1. In the first playoff game, my son tore his right ACL and was out for the rest of the season. It was mid-November and the doctor informed us that his recovery would take six months or more. He also stated that some recoveries are faster depending on the rehabilitation but he'd advise him to sit out the entire baseball season as well. **Can you say knocked off balance!**

My son was determined to recover in four months and be ready to play come mid-season. He worked out religiously and appeared to be about 80%. Nevertheless, the doctor was not releasing him and neither were we. More disappointments came and his grades slipped as well. As summer rolled around, he was ready to play. We were worried about him planting his feet, stopping quickly, and sliding, but he seemed to be fine. His summer league team had a good season, and he looked as though he was back to normal.

He was looking forward to his senior year. He realized that he had a potential college career in baseball and not football. So, he decided not to play football. When the baseball season began, there were a lot of new comers on the team. He was the captain and they looked up to him. As the coach tried to fill some key positions, he realized that he didn't have a solid short-stop. So, he decided to put my son there- again out of his comfort zone. Nevertheless, he was a team player and was willing to do whatever it takes. *"Individual commitment to a group effort-that is what makes a team work, a company work, a society work, a civilization work." (Inc.com).* **Hmmm....** **I am not feeling it. His recruitment chances are changing.**

He made a lot of mistakes at short-stop and it affected his confidence and batting. I told my wife and my son that I was going to talk with his coach and let him know that he has my son out of position and how it's affecting his confidence. My son didn't want me to do that. I informed him that it's going to affect your chances on playing college ball. He stated that "it's okay." Nevertheless, it was not okay. I bit my tongue at games when I'd see him struggle. *"For God gave us a spirit not of fear but of power and love and self-control. (2 Timothy 1:7).* It was good that I had that spirit, but I was bothered by my son's loss of confidence. Although I tried to keep him uplifted, my anger was still there.

The season ended, and it was a dismal one for my son and the team. It was a transitional season for the coach as well because the school didn't want him back after that year. See, I wasn't the only parent who complained about the coach. He had run off some good players and the parents knew their kids still wanted to play. My son was one of a few who decided to stick it out. He went on to college and it appeared that he was going to have an opportunity to play baseball, but he grew **impatient** with the process. He had to sit out a year from playing due to low test scores and clearing house. *"But if we hope for what we do not see, we wait for it with patience."* *(Romans 8:25)*. He dropped out the next year and has yet to return.

Dropping out of school didn't appear to cause him distress. He became a shift manager with a local restaurant. He met a pretty, young lady who became his girlfriend. He seemed happy and moving forward. Later, he rented an apartment with a friend. Things seemed to be going ok. Over the next year, he and his girlfriend would break up. His roommate, who never signed the lease, would move out. Now, he is left alone and paying all the bills. Financially, he was not able to maintain the apartment. He would break the lease agreement and move out. Just when he thought that he was branching out on his own, he had to move back in with mom! Poor decisions have left him feeling regret, used, and in debt. Now, he seems to be stuck in a rut. *"Trust in the Lord with all your heart, and do not lean on your own understanding. In all your ways acknowledge him, and he will make straight your paths."* *(Proverbs 3:5-6)*.

Over the last three years, he has lived with his mom and or dad. Both parents have offered him a chance to recover his finances and get back on track. But, he has taken both of us for granted. Wasting money and doing little for us. He acts as though he is **entitled** to what we are giving him. **Can you relate!** As we (his parents) give him stern talks on life and using opportunities and abilities to move forward, or maybe going back to school, he shuts down and avoid our conversations. We constantly inform him that the sky is the limit and you have to reach high. Nevertheless, **fear** and some **enablement** have limited his ability to soar.

Today, I have recommended some counseling but he doesn't feel as though he needs it. I think my writing and spiritual growth is helping him. He has chimed in on some topics in the book. Our conversations are better. He seems to be a little more motivated and stepping out of his comfort zone. He's taken on a second job and saving money. He now asks for more guidance and makes better decisions. Although I still encourage him to go back to school, he's doesn't have the desire. I also encourage him to pray but he's a little reluctant. Nevertheless, he's humble and slowly getting some balance in his life.

Anxiety Leading to Depression

Depression is a common and serious medical illness that

negatively affects how you feel, the way you think, and how you act. Depression causes feelings of sadness and/or a loss of interest in activities once enjoyed. It can lead to a variety of emotional and physical problems. <u>(American Psychiatric Association, January 2017).</u> Many people don't associate depression as a mental health issue because a lot of people who suffer from it are still functioning fine. So, it appears.

My youngest son has been battling anxiety and depression for 5 years. He was diagnosed in the spring of 2014. When he began to exhibit strange behaviors, and needed a mental evaluation, **it knocked us off balance**. Treatment would ensue. We couldn't believe this was happening. His future path had looked very bright. But, real life events triggered some mental instability. Although he is doing ok today, he had to put his most loved activity on hold, **baseball**, while he continues to cope and build his mental strength. It took a while for him to realize that there was a problem. He reminds me so much of myself.

Here's his story!

As a young child, he was a pure athlete-still is today. He was very fast in baseball, basketball, and football. During a span from age 6-12, many young athletes in the city of Nashville knew who he was. Many AAU coaches wanted him on their teams-especially basketball and baseball. He seemed to be a step above his peers. Not only was he a gifted athlete, he was smart, good manners, and loved by everyone. His friends were excited to be in his presence. He wasn't cocky and never tried to act better than anyone else. Now, he was spoiled and often got his way, but he was a good kid and seemed humble.

In the spring of 2010, things started changing. He and many of his baseball friends had joined an elite travel baseball team. He seemed super excited. The coach, who was a former MLB player, was fascinated by my son's natural hitting ability for a 12-year old. The coach had big plans for him and the team. Prior to working out on the baseball field, our son came home and said that he doesn't want to play with the team anymore. **What!!!** Why, we asked? He didn't like what the coach was doing or saying. **Hmmm…** Of course, I called the coach and ask what is going on. He replied that my son doesn't want to comply with his changes and he formed an attitude. The coach **was arrogant and a know it all**. Well, he didn't return to the team. He joined another team with less talent. I could tell it bothered him because he wasn't having fun.

Over the next 5 years, there would be a pattern and series of events. The following fall, he would try out for the middle school football team and quit. Basketball season begins, and he has a mediocre season. His mom and I separate, and I move out. His family structure has been **broken**. In the spring of 2011, I decide to coach his baseball team at Shelby park. It brought some excitement back and he had fun again and it was a great season. Summer AAU basketball season didn't seem to be as fun. He was bothered by his mistakes. His 8th grade year was interesting. He and the basketball coach didn't see eye to eye and he played sparingly. He began to talk back to teachers or make smart comments. He was about to be suspended from school for telling the assistant principal that *"rules are made to be broken"* when he was asked do you understand the rules. His behavior had changed and because of that, he had to start a debate team at school. He needs **counseling** and we don't realize it.

He loved baseball and basketball but didn't seem to be having fun anymore. Now, he's not getting the attention and support that he had gotten in the past from his parents. They are in separate households. We are losing trust, confidence, and money due to his starting and quitting activities. Many AAU coaches still know his potential, so they are paying for him to play. What a fortunate young man. Yet, he's not as humble as he was in earlier years. He's not giving the teams a good effort. *"Humble yourselves, therefore, under the mighty hand of God so at the proper time he may exalt you."* (1 Peter 5:6).

Well, 3 weeks before the start of school, we discovered that he didn't get into the same school as our middle son. The paperwork was not submitted on time. This meant that he would default to the high school in our zone. He was distraught and didn't want to attend this school. The school had a bad reputation and the sports programs were dismal-especially the baseball team. His mom and I told him that he would only have to attend for one semester. He hated it at first. He would skip school 4 times within two weeks. I wanted to discipline him physically, but he wasn't living with me and I wasn't sure if that would have helped.

He finally pulled it together. He had a couple of friends attending the school and they were excited that he was there. So were the coaches. The freshman football coach talked him into coming out and said that he'd be the quarterback for the team. He was excited, but he hadn't played in a couple years. After a few weeks of practice, the varsity coach was already talking about moving him up. He grew anxious and began to **fear failure**. So, he quit before the 1st game. I informed him that he must stop starting something and quitting. People will start to lose confidence in you.

Basketball season came around and he was ready. He led his freshman team in scoring, steals, and assists. The girls were crazy about him, but he had his eyes on one cheerleader and she had her eyes on him too. They became a couple. By January, he did not want to leave the school and attend the magnet school where his brother was. He decided to stay there instead. Baseball season begins, and he is one of the top players on the team. They won several games that year. The previous 3 years, the team didn't win a game. At the end of the season, I moved to NC. He and my middle son would spend the summer with me. It was a great summer with camps, swimming, baseball, and family events. They returned to Nashville to start school and everything seemed fine.

That fall basketball season, expectations were high for my son and the team. The coach was looking forward to my son taking charge just like he did the previous year. In early November, I flew into Nashville to visit him and my other two sons. I was hoping to see him playing basketball, but he had quit the team. When I asked him why, he responded that the coach was "tripping." The next day, I went to talk with the coach and asked what was going on. The coach replied, *"I wish I knew. He is a total different kid from last year. I informed him that he would be the player to guide our team to the state playoffs this year." He'd make mistakes, but they were all correctable. Yet, his demeanor showed that he wasn't pleased with himself. He seemed too anxious at times and struggled with the constructive criticism at practice." I know all his friends are on the JV team but he's one of the most talented of all the players on the varsity team. Plus, I think he's missing your presence.* **Wow! Does this sound a little familiar?**

It was my son's 10th grade year. He was dealing with peer pressure, the absence of his father, a nagging mom, spoiled, personal pressure, and tough homework assignments. He became anxious and over-whelmed. He struggled to overcome it. There were high expectations and he was **fearing failure**. I was able to help him some by association. I informed him of my struggles in 10th grade too. My conversations with him helped ease his mind and he went back to the basketball team. I had to return to North Carolina for work and I wished him well and told him to hang in there.

Within a month, he shuts down and quits the team again. He had put too much pressure on himself and couldn't deal with it. Although the coach was saying he played ok, my son was not agreeing with those words. He continued to struggle with the constructive criticism from the coach and his brothers. Oftentimes, telling his brothers to leave him alone. It began to affect his mental balance even more. He began to act out at home, skip school, not answer his phone, and seclude himself to his bedroom. I'd try to reach out to him, but he wouldn't talk. It would be a month and a half before I'd see him again (Christmas 2013).

In late January of 2014, he attended one of his high school basketball games. He seen how the team struggled and needed him. He began to feel as though he failed them. His friends would say, *"bruh they need you."* He'd leave the gym sad and feeling that he had let them down, but he knew that he couldn't handle the pressure. *"Blessed is the man who remains steadfast under trial, for when he has stood the test he will receive the crown of life, which God has promised to those who love him." (James 1:12).*

As the spring approached, he was super excited about baseball season. He was in good shape physically but mentally it was a wait and see. His instability didn't take long to come to light. Following the first tournament of the season, he didn't perform well and began to shut down again. **Wow**! He wouldn't go to practice and or school. My ex-wife and I discussed counseling again. This time she took him to Vanderbilt Adolescent center for help. He was diagnosed with anxiety, but no medicine needed. My son was smart and manipulative. I arrived in town just before his sessions were over. He was there a week and the counselors informed us that the coping sessions went well and that they were releasing him.

Within two weeks, my ex-wife called me and said he doesn't want to do anything. He's not going to school, nor his baseball games, he's pacing back and forth through the house, sleeping all day, abusing the animals in the house (cats and gerbils), and constantly making noise. He had even taken her car keys and attempted to drive himself somewhere but he had never driven before. He wouldn't give her the keys and began walking up and down the street, so she called the police. His actions had **knocked us off balance**. We couldn't understand what has happened to him.

When I returned to Nashville a couple weeks later, he had already missed four consecutive weeks of school. My ex-wife was stressed-rightfully so, and I was perplexed. Before this visit, he acted almost normal when I'd see him. This time, he appears to be distraught and fidgety. My ex-wife and I would coerce him into my truck and take him to a psychiatric center. It was painful taking him, but we wanted him to get more help. You never realized how tough mental illness is until it affects you and or your loved ones. He would remain in the treatment center for 8 consecutive days with only 2 visits during that timeframe. He was diagnosed with **anxiety and depression** and prescribed medication.

His psychiatrist informed us that our son was initially struggling with anxiety. As he tried to deal with it, other events started happening which put him in a depressive state. Because of that, he had shut down completely. Although he was not exhibiting some of the behaviors as other teens in the facility, he still needed some tests and evaluations. The doctor also stated that, even though our son doesn't appear to be suicidal or wanting to harm anyone, we don't always know their entire mental state. He also stated how he was missing his dad's presence and recommended that he lived with me. His mom was not so thrilled with that, but why wouldn't she be.

Upon release from the psychiatric center, our son went back to school and got some help making up his work. He had a great summer and played baseball again even though it wasn't recommended by the doctor. The doctor wanted him to take the summer off from baseball. Nevertheless, he played anyway. There were several backlashes in the fall and winter of 2014 and my ex-wife couldn't take it anymore. She wanted me to come get him. Although I wanted him to come live with me, it was not that easy. I arrived the weekend of Halloween and asked him was he ready to leave for NC with me. He said, "no." He didn't want to leave his environment, comfort zone, and his girlfriend. So, I reiterated to him about the importance of school, taking his medicine, going to counseling, and respecting his mom. I stressed that he needs to adhere to these things or come back with me. He agreed to adhere.

He continued taking the medicine, but he seemed more depressed when taking it. What he later told me was that he thought he heard someone talking in the house and felt that his grandfather's ghost was in there. See, his grandfather passed away in the house when he was 14. He wanted to get off the meds, but my ex-wife saw a positive difference when he was taking them. It was hard for me to tell a difference because I wasn't around him often enough.

Here are some of the things that came out of his counseling sessions:

As my son approached the adolescent years, he grew impatient. He wasn't getting the results fast enough. A new stage in life was occurring and he wasn't equipped to handle it. Expectations were higher, homework was harder, peer pressure was more present, status and social groups were forming, puberty was taking place, jealousy/envy was tugging at him. Things were not carefree and easy anymore. Now, he must work hard and earn those things that were once handed to him on a platter. He had become anxious.

*His psychiatrist stated that, just as he was beginning to adjust and cope with the anxiety, a series of events began to occur. His mom and dad separated. Dad moved across town. The home was filled with **gloom and brokenness**. Things got worse when his grandfather enters the home stricken with cancer and pass away in the house within a month. Three months later, his mom and dad's divorce was finalized and both seemed distant and sad. High school is starting but incomplete paperwork forced him to attend an underachieving high school with mediocre sports. He adjusts to the school environment but wonders how* *much better it would be if he was at another school. Then dad moves to North Carolina. **Separation anxiety** appears. His foundational structure became very unstable.*

*The 10th grade year rolls around. Expectations at the start of basketball season are very high. Pressure of maintaining **his status** is causing more anxiety. Constructive criticism from the coaches and critiquing from his brothers is upsetting him more. Mom is talking at him instead of talking to him. The comforting words from dad was not available. He becomes apprehensive with everything due to what he considers mistakes. Now, he begins to **fear failure**. As a result, he starts to shut down. Depression begins. Can you relate?*

A month after returning to NC, my ex-wife moves in with her boyfriend. This didn't appear to be an uncommon occurrence, but my son had to go with her. I didn't find out until Christmas and I didn't understand her rationale. What I assumed was she felt as though she needed some help with my son. She realized that he was not going to NC with his dad. The two of them were the only ones in the house. Oldest son was on his own and middle son was in college. She was constantly late for work because she wanted to ensure my son went to school. She had to force him to take his medicine at times. Plus, his behaviors were scary.

He was given an ultimatum. Either go live with your dad

in NC or move in with my boyfriend and me. **Wow!** I wasn't mad at my ex-wife for her decision, but I wished we had discussed it prior. My son was already **broken** and now he's removed from a place that is comfortable. He felt threatened to comply and forced to do something he didn't agree with. My ex-wife has always been a good mother and I appreciate that. Nevertheless, I didn't agree with her choice, but I wasn't in her place. She may have felt as though this was the best option. Plus, he was unstable, and she felt it was helpful and in the best interest for both. Upon visiting again for Christmas, my son said everything was going ok, but he seemed very sad. He said that it's different being away from the only home he's known. He stated that mom's boyfriend was cool. He mentioned that he was complying to everything, but his girlfriend is the one who's helping him cope.

I struggled to figure out how to help my son. I blamed myself for some of his challenges. His situation and conditions were affecting some of the balance in my personal life too. I wanted him to come live with me, but he had a choice. I didn't want to force him out of an environment that he was comfortable with. He knew that he wasn't in the most conducive situation, but he knew that he had to comply. I felt as though I left him, and his brothers **unprotected**. That I was a big part of his **brokenness**. I knew that he would be better if I was in his presence. He needed more than just my voice and quick visits. Plus, what I also realized was, so did I. I needed to be in arm lengths of all three of my boys. Although they were doing well when I left for NC, I started to feel as though I had abandoned them at vulnerable stages in their lives.

So, in the summer of 2015, I relocated back to Tennessee. My youngest son moved in with me immediately. He was ecstatic that I was back. I talked to his psychiatrist about teaching him to drive and he thought that was a great idea. So, he got his license in the early fall. He also had shoulder surgery in September and the recovery was six months. The recovery caused some backlash with anxiety. Going into his senior year of high school, he was being scouted as a perspective college baseball pitcher. We were warned by the doctor that the recovery would repair the damage but can't guarantee full strength and motion.

His senior year started off with a bang, he had 8 hits in his first 3 games. Although he wasn't ready to pitch until April, he continued to shine in center field and batting. On his first start as a pitcher, one of the college coaches came to see him pitch. Well, feeling a little anxious, he tried to impress the coach and his performance wasn't dismal. Plus, his shoulder was hurting. I could see his disappointment and I worried about his reaction. This time around, I am present to help him cope with disappointments. I encouraged him to keep moving forward. He knew that he was well supported.

He lost a lot of interest in college scouts because they wanted him to pitch and he couldn't. His arm strength was not there yet, and coaches didn't want to take that chance. Although he was bothered, he persevered and lit it up offensively. He finished his senior year with a batting average of .600 which was at the top in the state. He also was in the top 10 in 3 other offensive categories. Unfortunately, many colleges had already scouted and selected their recruits. He remained humble and was offered to play junior college baseball at Volunteer State Community College. They were excited to have gotten a player like him. They felt as though they had a steal and couldn't wait till the start of the season.

Well, he struggled adjusting to the college life, strict agendas with baseball, fitting in time with his girlfriend, and homework. During early fall practice, he was back to putting too much pressure on himself to perform. He wasn't hitting well and was upset at himself. His throws in the field were off target and his arm started to hurt. The coach told him not to worry, that he would adjust. My son grew impatient and was ready to quit. *"And let us not grow weary of doing good, for in due season we will reap, if we do not give up." (Galatians 6:9).* I couldn't persuade him to hang in there this time. Once again, the expectations he envisioned were high and he **feared failure** and he didn't want to allow it to put him in a state of depression.

Today, he's continuing his education. He spends a lot of time with his girlfriend for which that relationship is leading to the **ultimate goal**. He hasn't found resolve for leaving the game of baseball, but his mental state is stable. I, like many others, would love to see him on the field again, but I'm thankful that he's doing well and getting his education. Although he is a spiritual young man and trust in the Father Almighty, he's slowly incorporating daily prayer. He finds balance through work, school, assisting at homeless shelters, and spending time with his girlfriend. Upon graduating from college, he desires to become an entrepreneur and a coach. He also realizes that his abilities extend well beyond baseball.

As you can see, I believe God sent me back to Tennessee to help each one of my boys. When my divorce occurred, it left each one of them uncovered. Although they had took flight as good young men, they had not reached the height to soar like eagles. They all still needed some fatherly guidance. For 14, 16, and 22 years, all they seen was mom, dad, and family together. When we separated and divorced, that foundation was damaged and they were left trying to take on fatherly duties around the house, school, peer pressure, work, life, etc. Plus, their mom and or dad was not accessible as before. Life coaching and or counseling was needed and they couldn't get it all from mom and dad. We assumed that they would all be ok.

Preparation for life challenges, obedience to God, and guidance from their father was missing. Yet, Satan's deceptions were present. Not that their mom couldn't provide guidance for them, because she was doing what she could! Now, I don't have all the answers either but I've found trust in God. *"I will instruct you and teach you in the way you should go; I will counsel you with my eye upon you. (Psalm 32:8).* We still have some mountains to climb but we realize that now we all have spikes on our shoes that allows us to dig in as we climb to the top.

Depression leading to Suicide

A couple months after moving back to Nashville, I met a lady at the bar area of Logan's restaurant. That friendly encounter turned into a long conversation. Neither of us were looking for anyone or anything but it's was something special about the connection. I told her I that I recently moved back to the area. When I told her my purpose for the move, it struck an accord. She was emotionally moved. She'd go on to tell me about some **unexpected events that changed her life.** She had lost her father and her only son to suicide because of depression only one year apart. Can you say **knocked off balance**!

As her son went through his elementary school years, she states that he exhibited some anger issues and she couldn't understand why. He was a good kid, smart, and spiritually inclined. His anger came when other students were acting out in class. He would get mad at them for disrupting class. Consequently, his words to them would incite arguments and fights and get himself in trouble. She would move him to 2 other schools during those years because the teachers said that he had behavior issues. **Wow! Can you relate?**

She would enroll him into a *Community Action Project(Y-CAP) sponsored by the YMCA*. It is a program to help students facing greater challenges achieve that potential by providing the coaching, mentoring, hands on experience, and resources they need to succeed. He loved the program and enjoyed helping others. He would see the same joy and passion from his grandfather in church. See, his grandfather was a minister and he loved to teach people the word of God. Her son adored and looked up to his grandfather. He was a very structured man and took great pride in taking care of his family.

As years passed, her son had blossomed into an outstanding football player in high school. Her dad, the grandfather, was proud of his grandson but was unable to see him play. He had become stricken with **Diabetes** and it had taken his eyesight. Losing his eyesight had put him into a state of depression. Because he couldn't see, he was unable to read his bible. He became apprehensive of going to church when he couldn't do what he has done best for nearly 40 years. He felt as though he couldn't teach without seeing the people. He couldn't drive anymore or do things around the house. He felt less than a man and **feared failure**. As a minister and a man of God, he knew that he shouldn't fear anything. *"For God gave us a spirit not to fear but of power and love and self-control."* *(2 Timothy 1:7)*. He wasn't feeling that spirit anymore and felt his life was now worthless and purposeless. Because of that feeling, he shot and killed himself in one of the closets of his home. **Can you say knocked off balance!**

This event was a devastating blow to the entire community. It would change many lives. It would also show loved ones and friends how one's life can be shattered within the **blink of an eye**. His family knew he was depressed but never imagined that he would take his own life. Her son took it very hard. He'd lost a great grandfather and a great confidant. Although his grandfather was unable to see him play football, he'd often call him for advice and guidance following a bad game. He'd also confide in him when dealing with relationships, disagreements with his parents, teachers, and coaches.

A year later, her son needed his grandfather's words of encouragement. Although he grew up in a two- parent household, he didn't confide in his parents like he did with his grandfather. Nevertheless, his parents were always there for him. At the start of his senior year, excitement and expectations were high. The previous year, he and the coach had talked about a few colleges that were interested in him playing for them. Well, that coach was no longer there. The new coach had plans of restructuring the team and her son's role was not going to be the same as the previous two years. Because of those plans, he and the coach were not seeing eye to eye. The new structure was not going to garnish the looks from those colleges that showed interest in him.

As the season started, he went from a starting linebacker to playing sparingly. He and the coach would argue after games. Finally, the coach felt as though her son was disrupting the team. So, he dismissed him from the team. **Wow!** It brought shockwaves to her son, to her and her husband, and to the team. How could this be happening to one of the best players on the team. He didn't know what to do. His status had completely changed. He didn't want to go to school and or work anymore. He was tired of people asking him what happened. He was secluding himself to his room and didn't want to be bothered. He had become depressed.

Granddaddy was not available to help him.

Through prayer, love, and encouragement from his parents and friends, he'd pick himself up. So, it seemed. Football season was over and in his mind, so was his career as a football player. He'd go back to school and work. Hang out occasionally with friends but still secluded himself to his room! His friends would tell him where certain athletes were attending college next year. They didn't realize that it bothered her son, but it did. She asked him if he'd like to go and talk to someone(counseling) but he declined. She wished that she had just taken him anyway. One evening as she arrived home from work, she noticed his car was there, but he told her he was working after school. As she came into the house and called his name, he didn't answer. She heard the TV playing in his room and knocked on the door but no answer. Upon opening the door, he appeared to be asleep. When she shook him to wake him up, she saw blood on his pillow. She felt his arms and they were ice cold. She saw a gun on the floor. Her son had committed suicide. **Wow! Can you say knocked off balance!**

Depression had taken the lives of two of her most dear loved ones-only a year apart. She'd say, *"how did God allow this to happen to two of his children."* In *2 Samuel 17:23*, the bible references how Ahithophel put everything in his home in order before taking his life. He feared failure. Life seemed hopeless and purposeless. Is this what happened with her father and son? She would struggle for a while. She'd go into a state of depression too. Fortunately, she would pray and seek counseling. She'd also take some medicine to help her cope and get through each day. Although she struggled with the events, she stated that she was not going to allow depression and the devil keep her down.

Today, she is a member of the Tennessee Suicide Prevention Network. They often call upon her to speak at conferences concerning suicide prevention. This gives her a chance to tell her story in hopes of helping others. She also speaks at churches and schools. She contends that her faith in God has guided her to find strength and the courage to share her story.

What is Anxiety and Depression doing to you or people in your circle? Are you seeking help before the conditions worsen? How are you coping with it? Do you realize that you are suffering from anxiety or depression? Just because you are functioning at home or on the job, does not mean that you can't be in depression. What kind of help and advice are you seeking or giving? Are you apprehensive of seeking help because you fear being labeled as unstable? Are you fearing failure in life? When entitlement is no longer, how are you reacting? When expectations are high, what state of mind does it put you in?

Are your kids anxious because they feel that they can't measure up to your standards?

Think about your current situation or someone in your circle who are struggling with these challenges! How will you find resolve or advise others? Should prayer be a part of it? What are the triggers to your imbalance? I have found that a good starting point to diagnosing one's mental instability is recognizing that a problem exists. Don't be afraid to seek help! *"Ask, and it will be given to you; seek, and you will find; knock, and it will be opened to you." (Matthew 7:7).*

PTSD

The Mayo Clinic describes this condition as a disorder characterized by failure to recover after experiencing or witnessing a terrifying event. Although this disorder is more common with soldiers following war, it affects many others who have been hit with a traumatic blow.

As you recall from several of the previous chapters, there were events that occurred with family members and or my circle that could lead to PTSD. I think that my oldest sister suffered the most amongst the siblings. Sitting beside her husband as he was shot and killed caused instability for the remainder of her life. Although she received treatment, it couldn't heal her. She didn't speak much about the traumatic event, but it was obvious how it affected her.

You also heard how one of my good friends suffers from PTSD following the Fort Hood shooting. Although he has adjusted well since the event, he has his moments-especially during the anniversary years. Without a doubt, it appears that people learn to cope following a traumatic event, but the affects leave mental scars for the rest of their lives. The suffering never completely subsides. *"Those who suffer, he delivers in their suffering; he speaks to them in their affliction." (Job 36:15).*

Do you remember that daughter who came into the room and asked Mr. Scott, *"where are you going daddy?"* Well, she needed some help following that abandonment. Although it may not be the type of traumatic experiences to cause PTSD, it had a traumatizing effect on her. In fact, over 50 years later, she still recalls that day. She recovered well following treatment and would go on to live a normal life.

In the fall of 1991, she would not only witness one of the most horrific events, she would be a victim as well. There was an explosion and a huge fire in the poultry plant she worked in. Twenty-five lives were lost from this event. She made it out of the fire but suffered minor burns and severe smoke inhalation. She recalls the pushing and shoving as they all tried to get out of the building. She had stepped over victims who passed out from the smoke. She saw colleagues burned to death trying to get out of the door. **Can you say knocked off balance!** Not only did this event take the lives of people, it changed the lives of many more.

As people tried to exit the building, two of the three doors had been chained with a lock from the outside. Apparently, there had been some theft of chicken on previous days and the plant management team had the doors chained without notifying the teammates. **Wow!** See the book, *The Hamlet Fire: A Tragic Story of Cheap Food, Cheap Government, and Cheap Lives* by Bryant Simon. Many lawsuits would follow. The plant would be shut down and the plant manager would go to prison. The plant was eventually torn down and it is now a memorial site for the victims.

You can imagine the healing and counseling that was needed for the victims and their families. Also, the entire town needed the same. Not only was there a lot of grieving, people in the community were very angry. They couldn't believe what the management of the facility had done, the slow response from the EMS and Fire department, and the negative publicity from the media. The entire community was off balance. *"For the anger of man does not produce the righteousness of God." (James 1:20).*

My sister was ok physically but It would take a while to

heal mentally. She, like other victims, would receive as much counseling as needed. Of course, she would get a lot of love and support from family and friends too. Following the funerals, she was invited to speak at a conference in Washington D.C on behalf of herself and some of the other victims. As months passed, she struggled to overcome some of the trauma. Nightmares about the event would haunt her for a long time. She had to take some medications to help her relax and cope throughout the day. She would also see a therapist once a week. Her therapist insisted that she surround herself with family and or friends to keep from being detached. Her kids and boyfriend worked hard to keep her mind off of the event by engaging in other activities. She stated that she prayed each night as well. Mom worried about her and called often.

Today, she continues to take medicine to help her relax. She still has occasional nightmares but not necessarily about the fire. She can't remember most of them but her loved ones have stated that there's screams and fighting. Nevertheless, she continues to do what she loves the most, which is cooking. **That is on burners, not over flames.** She has also taken over as the **matriarch** of our family. She is the oldest living sibling and one we all go to for family knowledge and history. She is a humble woman who's always helping others but asking for nothing in return. We have multiple gatherings at her home each year and she can't wait to cook something. She thanks God for giving her a new perspective on life and never take it for granted. She realizes that her life was spared from that unexpected event.

Chapter 15

Spirituality (Struggles with Sin and Christian Life)

My mother was not a saint, but she was an angel-at least in our eyes. Unfortunately, her wings were damaged early in life. She was not able to soar like an eagle. She had flaws just like you and I have. Nevertheless, mom still desired to live a Christian life. Although she wasn't going to church on a regular basis, she prayed every night and tried to follow the life of a Christian. When she was abandoned by her husband, the devil began to hover around her and the family. Her husband did not build a solid foundation for her and the kids. Because of that, the walls began to cave in.

After mom had exhausted all the help from family and friends, she had to result to some unfaithful measures to support her kids, but she prayed to God for forgiveness. That support came with a cost that took her away from her spiritual beliefs. She was criticized, judged, and labeled by friends and church members. She felt ostracized and betrayed. When judgement came from the church, she was reluctant to seek their help. She prayed to God for help, but it appeared Satan was intercepting many of her pleas.

"Rescue the weak and the needy, deliver them from the hand of the wicked." (Psalm 82:4).

For most of us, we believe that we live in the greatest country in the world. Our country is the land of the free. We are a loving, caring, supportive, and looking out for our neighbors, kind of country, right. We have strong Christian values too, right. Then, why are we so quick to judge others? Look down on them because of their shortcomings or the way they look! Would you say that many of us are hypocritical? In general conversation, many of us are often talking about someone else. Judging them on what they are doing, not doing, or have done! Should many of us even have the audacity or do we consider it discernment? *"Do not judge by appearances, but judge with the right judgement." (John 7:24).*

Many of us act, as though, our lives are so much better than others. Many of us believe that because of our position, status, or finances, it propels us to a potentially higher Christian life. Some believe that because they attend a bigger church with a well-known minister makes them a better Christian. How about being in a certain denomination? Does that make you a better Christian? Why is that? How often do you meet someone and they ask "what church do you attend?" When you tell them, they respond, "I've never heard of that one." As though, it really matters. If we all worship the same God and going to church, then it doesn't matter about the name, size, minister, or denomination?

Many people in our country believe that sins committed by those of higher status is less severe than those of low status. Can you relate? Sin is sin, right. I don't recall the bible stating that Jesus died for the sins of the rich, the priests, attorneys, doctors, and or other professionals. *"He is the propitiation for our sins, and not for ours only but also for the sins of the whole world." (1 John 2:2)*. Do you realize that many of us are constantly sinning every day and think nothing of it? Furthermore, we're not asking for forgiveness. Some believers say they have repented of their sins but are back to doing the same things two months later. Can you imagine how life would be if God punished all for their sins and magnified the punishment for those who have repented and sinning again!

I recall family and friends saying that I am a Godly man. They said I was nice, generous, always giving support, and encouragement. They said that I and my brother, El, were "naturally sharpened" by God (Uncommon Life, Tony Dungy June 30). I was also told that I do a great job of taking care of my family and is totally involved with my boy's activities. Plus, I attend church on a regular basis. They admired me for that. Wow! Those are some nice words, right. I may have seemed to

Walk the Talk, but I didn't **Walk with God**. Yes, I was going to church on the regular basis, but I wasn't getting anything out of it. I wasn't a part of the men's choir nor any ministries. I had yet to become obedient. *"I have chosen the way of faithfulness; I set your rules before me." (Psalm 119:30).* I knew I wasn't following all the rules but didn't realize that I was so far off. Can you relate?

I've exhibited envy of others. I've been judgmental at times. I've had lustful feelings and became an adulterer when I was married. *"But I tell you that anyone who looks at a woman or man lustfully has already committed adultery with them in their hearts." (Matthew 5:28).* **Wow! This is a tough one, huh.** Are we admiring and complimenting the beauty or the body? Can you relate?

I was not exemplifying a Christian life, but I was still accepted and looked up to by others. Yeah, I know none of us are perfect but which life are you going to live. I had a wonderful family, but I wasn't setting a good example. Satan's deception had me thinking that my behaviors weren't so bad. *"So, because you are lukewarm, neither hot nor cold, I will spit you out of my mouth." (Revelation 3:16).* Which life are you living? Many of us are worshipping God on Sunday, yet sinning all other days of the week. I know people who think they are more of a Christian than I am because they can reference more scriptures from the bible than I can. Is it better to know scriptures or know and follow God? Is it better to attend service or serve the Lord? Is it better to know scriptures or follow the path?

Recently, I watched one of my all-time favorite movies, _Seven_, _starring Morgan Freeman and Brad Pitt._ The movie portrayed a deranged serial killer who is targeting people he thinks are representing one of the seven deadly sins (**Gluttony, Sloth, Greed, Pride, Lust, Wrath, Envy**). When I first saw the movie in the mid-90's, I was a young newlywed and happy with life. It was a good movie but didn't get a lot out of it because of the place I was in. Now, I wasn't spiritually inclined, but I was doing the right things. Today, the movie has more meaning and more visibility. Take a moment to think about these sins! How are they affecting your life and balance? Did you imagine that you may be committing some of these sins?

Do you realize that many countries despise us because of the first three sins listed above? Some envy us for the freedoms, liberty, and financial opportunities as well. There's built up tension and anger because they feel we are ungrateful and hypocritical. Yet, many of us call ourselves Christians. A lot of these feelings have led to despicable hatred, violence, and terrorist attacks. _"But now you must put them all away: anger,_

wrath, malice, slander, and obscene talk from your mouth."
(Colossians 3:8).

I've witnessed sin often, I have committed sins, and become a victim of the sins. It appears, as though, sin is incorporated in many of our everyday lives. Not that we want to be labeled a sinner, but it's widely accepted. Most of us know that it's not the Christian way of life. Some of us also feel that what one doesn't know, won't hurt them. We all realize that there could be some serious consequences to our actions; yet, we are still willing to take that risk.

When I met my girlfriend, she had been out of the marriage for sixteen months. She was ready for a serious relationship. Now, I thought it was very soon to want something serious after being out of marriage for only a short period of time. There was still a lot of unfinished business between her and her ex-husband. Plus, she has a teenage daughter at home who is still in high school. Six months into our relationship, things are going well. We are meeting each other's kids, enjoying entertainment, and taking weekend excursions.

Every now and then, the ex-husband would send her and their kids little innuendos by text messaging as though it was bothering him that she was looking happy. **(Envy)**. Plus, he had found me on Facebook, copied pictures, and sent them to her. He also sent pictures of some women whom he thought were beautiful as though he was showing a comparison. Why? My girlfriend was very reluctant to tell me about his behavior, but she thought that I needed to know. **Was he jealous?** In his church, he's viewed as a man of God.

One Sunday in March, she called me at work and said that she had cooked dinner and would like for me to come by when I get off. When I arrived, she was the only one at home and dinner with wine was on the table. Upon finishing dinner, I complimented her on the wonderful meal. I also told her how beautiful she was. We would go into the living room and sit in a chair. She'd straddle my legs and sit in my lap hugging and kissing me. As we began to get intimate (**Lust, Fornication**), I joked with her about her ex-husband or someone else looking in the window and seeing us naked. See, there are long, rectangular shaped windows that run along- side her front door. Well, it turns out that we should be careful with the jokes.

Fifteen minutes later, we'd hear the entry door from the garage open. She jumps up from my lap and yells, "wait a minute son." She thought it was her oldest son. In comes her ex-husband. She's completely naked and I'm in only socks and t-shirt. As she screams, "what are you doing here", I manage to pull my underwear up. He's yelling about his things in the house and his name still on the deed. He continues to call her names and say you're disrespecting the house, but it's now her house. **(Wrath).** He turns to me and say, "this is not about you Scott." Then he swings at me. The punch misses and we wrestle to the floor. Kicking and punching is occurring, and I yell to my girlfriend to call the police.

As she goes up the stairs to retrieve her phone, he gets off me and goes after her. I put on my pants and go out the door looking for a weapon on the porch. I would call 911 while looking at the 2 of them on the stairs. At first, I thought he was hitting her, so I went to my truck to see if I had a baseball bat inside. When I came back to the front door, he had his phone out taking pictures of her naked body. As I started to come in, he came after me outside. This time, he swings and misses again.

Amid the fight, my thoughts of being a boxer in my teenage years had come full circle. See, in middle school and high school, I loved boxing. Oftentimes, me and the guys would slap box in the halls and gym. I was super quick with my hands as I emulated Muhammed Ali and Sugar Ray Leonard. I had gained much respect from friends who wanted to try my quick hands. I realized that I had an advantage on most of them because I was ambidextrous. They were only one-handed. I'd wait for them to swing with their dominate hand, then I'd swing and hit them twice before they could react. They'd lose their balance.

As my girlfriend's ex swung with his lazy right hand, I'd strike him twice in the face. As he stumbles, I'd push him head first into the wooden railings of the porch-breaking the rails. He would get up from the ground and go to his truck. He yells back at his ex-wife, "get the house out of my name", and takes off. **Wow! Can you say unexpected event that knocks you off-balance, literally!**

While sitting on the couch and awaiting the police, my girlfriend and I look at each other and ask, "are you ok?" We both reply, "yes." She then asks me, "are you going to leave me-meaning the relationship?" I reply, "let's not think about that right now." To get her mind off that statement, I'd say, "I better stop joking about shit, because it comes true." Then we both laugh. After giving our statements to the police and getting checked by EMS, she files a warrant for his arrest. She felt bad that she had to result to that but realize that her ex-husband needs some help. To add to her justification, she receives text messages from him with naked pictures of her on my lap and on the stairs. He had sent the same pictures to her three children as well. **Wow! Are these the actions of a man of God?**

Can you imagine how serious this event could have been? (jealous rage resulting in murder, murder suicide, what if I found a weapon or had a gun in my truck). What could have happened if he'd got up from the ground and continued to try and fight me. Now, it's truly self-defense. Any such reaction could have changed the course of our lives or our families lives forever. *"Anger is cruel, and fury is overwhelming, but who can stand before jealousy." (Proverbs 27:4)*. Although I'm not the most spiritual person in the world, I believe that a higher power didn't want me to find a weapon that night.

Today, my girlfriend and I are still together. I told her to take care of all her unfinished business and family matters. Don't rush to get serious with me because I'm in no hurry! I'd tell her that I was pulling back a little to allow her time to take care of things, but I am not going anywhere. I would also say that "although I'm not fearful, I shouldn't have to walk around wondering if someone is going to attack us." *"You will be hidden from the scourge of the tongue, and you will not be afraid of violence when it comes. (Job 5:21)*. Although things are going well, she realizes that my guard is up. Not because of fearing another attack but wondering if business and family affairs will improve or worsen. Since this event, we have started to pray together. Plus, we have incorporated reading devotionals every day.

It bewilders me that jealousy, envy, anger, and strife cause so much hate in our world. Love, understanding, resolving conflict, and or settling differences seem non-existent at times. If we are true Christians, we wouldn't be exhibiting such behaviors. But, we tend to hate our neighbors because of their color/nationality, opinions, religious beliefs, their positions, their walk of life, etc. Surely, people who are part of hate groups don't believe they are Christians or do they. Why? Although we all came from the same maker, God knew there would be challenges. Plus, Satan, with his deception, would be lurking around trying to lure the confused. *"Whomever hates disguises himself with his lips and harbors deceit in his heart, when he speaks graciously, believe him not, for there are seven abominations in his heart, though his hatred be covered with deception, his wickedness will be exposed in the assembly." (Proverbs 26:24-26).*

According to the dictionary, **spirituality** *is the quality of being concerned with the human spirit or soul as opposed to material or physical things. Wikipedia also describes Spirituality as being the religious process of re-formation which aims to recover the original shape of man oriented at the image of God.* Of course, the meaning or interpretation is much broader than these definitions. Some people believe in God and consider themselves spiritual but not necessarily religious. They don't believe that they must follow religious rituals to be considered a Christian. Can you relate? What is your current spiritual position?

Traditionally, spiritual or religious upbringing has fostered positive results in behaviors/attitudes, school achievements, relationships, marriages, work, understanding, etc. Although we can draw that same conclusion today, things have changed significantly. We are accepting things that are considered abominations in the bible. Yet, we judge and label those who are changing their lives to walk with God. Are these behaviors some of the new, approved Christian concepts? Think about it for a moment! We have accepted and chosen what not to speak on but continue to judge others for following a Christian life. *"If anyone sins in that he hears a public adjuration to testify, and though he is a witness, whether he has seen or come to know the matter, yet does not speak, he shall bear his iniquity." (Leviticus 5:1).* Nevertheless, none of us are perfect and asking for forgiveness should become constant.

In the summer of 2016, I ran across another friend from college as I was leaving the gym. She was surprised to see me but in a hurry to get to her yoga class. I told her that I was divorced and now live in the area. I didn't think much more about the meeting until she reached out to one of my nephews on Facebook trying to get in touch with me. I was flabbergasted with her attempts to reach me. Nevertheless, I got the information from my nephew and called her. The conversations were good, but I could tell that we were in a different place spiritually. She was bothered by my sexual encounters over the past five years and she told me that we need to have a conversation with God. Hmmm.......

See, eight years prior, she had become stricken with cancer and thought that she was going to die. She was struggling to fight because she thought there was not much to live for. She wasn't married, didn't have a boyfriend, nor did she have any kids. She had family, but they were all distant. She realized that her illness would leave her broke and in debt. She told me how she prayed to God for strength, courage, guidance, and purpose. *"Wait for the Lord, be strong, and let your heart take courage; wait for the Lord." (Psalms 27:14).* She would build up strength and after a year of treatment and prayer, her cancer would go into remission.

Following her recovery, she believed that her calling was to spread the word of God and tell what he had done for her. So, she sold her house and enrolled in a Seminary school in North Carolina. Her family was skeptical of her choice, but it wasn't for them. Nevertheless, she would earn a degree in Theology. Uncertain on getting started into the ministry, she would patiently wait on God's direction. Her resume now includes a BBA, MBA, certified accountant, and a Theological degree. Finding a job was not an issue for her!

Over the next three years, she would take a job in Ohio as an accountant for a law firm and build up her finances. She would also build her first home. She would join a local church and start several ministries for women. The ministries would discuss abstinence and sexual purity, marriage, submission, individuality, and independence. She was well received by the women of the church, but she was bothered by their admission to **fornication** despite the messages. At this point in her life, she said that she had been abstinent for twenty years. Whew! She decided to move back to Tennessee in 2014. She is financially comfortable and build another home. She is still single but interested in getting married one day and have kids, but she remains patient. As she contemplated on her career path, she would spend time with her new church and her niece and nephew. Her brother and his wife lived a few miles from her and she'd often offer to babysit for them. Her niece and nephew were elementary age kids with a lot of energy and intuitiveness. She is loving the time spent with them and so are they. They would play, go to museums, read spiritual books, and watch spiritual children's plays. She would cook for them too.

She discovered that she had a love for cooking and baking. She would befriend neighbors and have them trial her food. A couple of them were impressed with her baking goods and suggested she start her own business. She was appreciative of the compliments but reluctant on starting a business. As she baked cakes and bread for local functions and her churches, people began to offer her money to bake for them. So, she decided to use her financial background and start her own business. Again, family members didn't like her idea, but they have seen first-hand how she as persevered. She would invite friends over to try her baked goods before selling them. She'd also take samples to her favorite neighbors-a married couple whom she called beautiful people.

Suddenly, the struggle with sins vs living a Christian life comes to the forefront or maybe Satan intervenes. Her visits to her favorite neighbor's home were occurring when the wife was not at home. The husband comes to the door without a shirt. During previous visits, she had complimented the husband on how handsome he was. The wife begins to feel a little anxious that she brings things over when she's not there. Some of her family and friends become jealous and envy of her home, cars, business, and high-spirited attitude. Her mom is upset that she will not loan her money and tells her that God will make a way for her. Her brother and his wife discover that she was exposing their kids to spirituality without their permission. Do you remember from a previous chapter the person who told her married friends to get an extra **orgasm** for her? Well, here she is. A couple of her girlfriends would tell her that she needs to let her guard down a little to catch that man. (**Fornication**). Wow! Everyone appears to be out of order.

Within a few months, her favorite neighbors don't want her to come around anymore. The next-door neighbor has taken her to court over the property landline. Her brother and his wife have labeled her as crazy and won't allow her to see the kids anymore. The kids are confused. Her own mom talks down about her to other family members who now think that she is crazy too. Those two girlfriends who encourage her to let her guard down have distance themselves after she put them in their place. **Can you say knocked off balance!** Although it wasn't enough to change her course of life, she put it in God's hands. *"And we know that those who love God, all things work together for good, for those who are called according to his purpose." (Romans 8:28)*.

Today, her baked bread business is doing well. She devotes a lot of her time to the church and is slowly getting involved in sermons. She's back to overseeing several women's ministries. Even though she has apologized to her brother and his wife, they still don't allow her to babysit anymore but she gets to see her niece and nephew from time to time. Her mother has since apologized for her actions, but it hasn't changed how other family member view her. She has let go of those disparaging friends but has not let down her guard. That special man has yet to find her, but she doesn't allow it to dampen her spirit. *"He who finds a wife finds a good thing and obtains favor from the Lord." (Proverbs 18:22).*

Think about your current situation! What spiritual place are you in today? Are you struggling with sin and spirituality? Do you realize that you are sinning? Do you ask for forgiveness? How is sin affecting your balance? Do you fear being judged or labeled by others because of your walk? Are you sacrificing your beliefs to be accepted into certain groups? Are you apprehensive to pray and ask for guidance? Have you accepted sin as common practice? Although Jesus died for our sins, does it mean that it's impossible to live a Christian life?

Conclusion

My mother wanted a marriage full of love, support, guidance, protection, discipline, submission, spirituality, and more. Unfortunately, what she got was the total opposite. Mr. Scott left her, and the kids uncovered. It gave the devil an opportunity to climb through the window. He brought with him anxiety, fear, rape, shame/embarrassment, loneliness, and invasion. All these things would add to more dysfunction in the family. Through prayer and the grace of God, mom would persevere. Although she endured a lot of obstacles along the way, she remained *"steadfast and immovable, always abounding in the work of the Lord." (Corinthians 15:58)*. Mom knew that she had to weather the storm despite the torrential downpours. Now, we all want to praise mom for her courage and strength; but for her, it wasn't about *"how strong she was, it was being strong was her only choice" (Bob Marley)*.

What are your relationship goals? Make them clear with whomever you are pursuing! No one wants to be hurt, misled, or misunderstood. Despite potential disappointments, open and honest communication are always good. At least you'll know what to expect. There are consequences to lies and hidden agendas. Are you willing to take those risks? The desire to be in a committed relationship which leads to the ultimate goal seem to be lost in many socio-economic groups. Why? Eventually, most of us will reach a point in our lives for which the same old pattern will end. If we're not careful, we'll be labeled, judged, sick, and **alone**.

Mr. Scott had a *Proverbs 31* woman. She intended to be obedient and submissive. She was a beautiful woman and wanted to be loved. She was a **dime piece**. Most of us men would have loved to have a woman like mom. He knew what he had but he deceived her. She thought that she had a **Prince Charming** but he turned out to be a **frog**. He was corrupted by Satan and pretended to want a marriage. In essence, he prevented her from a relationship of marital bliss.

Marriage is a divine commitment. Don't' take it for granted! I learned the hard way. It's a great idea to seek pre-marital counseling before jumping that broom. True love should be the #1 reason that we get married. If there is uncertainty, then maybe it's not time or not the right person to marry. Getting married for the wrong reasons comes with a lot of risks and consequences! Remember that woman was pulled from the rib of a man to be the perfect match and lifetime companion! Yeah, we know that the perfect one may not be out there, but a good match is. Honor your vows and stay true to your marriage! *"Therefore, a man should leave his father and mother and hold fast to his wife, and the two shall become of one flesh." (Ephesians 5:31).*

When those vows are broken, the trust is gone, and recovery seems impossible. Then decide your course of action! It's okay to pray and ask God for guidance. Before we divorce, we all must be 100% sure that's it's beyond repair. Some circumstances may be unbearable, and divorce is the best solution. Unquestionably, marriage should be until death do us part, but the marriage situation should not kill us. So, ask God for forgiveness and do what's in the best interest of all! If you all decide to work it out, you should do your own repentance to each other. Your past behaviors and transgressions should not appear in the 2nd chance marriage. Have clear communication with expectations! Compromise and resolve your disagreements when they occur! If it doesn't work out, don't hate each other for the failure. Forgive and move forward!

Looking back, not only did my marriage problems and divorce take a toll on my life, it had a major effect on my sons too. Their foundational structure was damaged. They were somewhat neglected during our marital battles. They didn't know how to respond or if they should intervene. They were apprehensive when approaching us about things they needed. The divorce was devastating to all of us and we all should have sought counseling too. Although all three of my boys seemed fine when I left for NC, the move was at a pivotal, transitional time for all of them. I didn't give that much thought. When depression hit my youngest son, I felt as though I had abandoned them, almost like Mr. Scott did with mom. I needed to train them up more before letting them soar. *"Train up a child in the way he should go; even when he is old, he will not depart from it." (Proverbs 22:6).*

Nearly 15% of Americans live below the poverty line. Although demographics, education, health, and generational poverty are all key factors; choice, situational, and fear are reasons as well. Many children who grow up in poverty are more susceptible to malnutrition, poor health and hygiene, low self-esteem, behavior issues, learning disabilities, violence, etc. Most come from single parent and dysfunctional households. A lot of them live in high crime communities as well. With that said, the chance of success and breaking the generational cycle is low.

Many children who are raised by selfless and spiritual inclined parents or grandparents seem to have a greater chance of surviving poverty. Nevertheless, paving the way does not always reap rewards. Mom was selfless and spiritually inclined but she never had a solid foundation. She tried her best to guide her children in the right direction. She knew that staying on the path with God and ignoring the distractions, would bring positive results! *"But seek first the kingdom of God and his righteousness, and all these things will be added to you."* *(Matthew 6:33).* Taking advantage of opportunities, staying driven, and getting a good education is key to breaking the cycle.

Early in my life, I didn't realize that I had a mental disturbance. It wasn't anything serious and I was still functioning fine. Nevertheless, it was causing some nervousness, fear, apprehensions, amongst other things. I persevered because of determination, but it could have easily gone the other way. Things fell in place for me with graduation, marriage, and a solid job. It wasn't so easy for my youngest son. His foundational structure was damaged during a pivotal time in his life and he struggled to move forward. As years progressed, more and more events begin to occur. Counseling was needed early in his life and we didn't realize it. Contrarily, my other two sons needed counseling too.

What happens to others when there's mental instability and a chain of unexpected events occur in their lives? Don't wait to seek help and or guidance! Don't just talk about your loved ones and friends! Try to help them! What about yourself? Do you realize that you may be a functional depressant? If you're not spiritually prepared and or praying, the next unexpected event could throw you over the top. *"When the righteous cry for help, the Lord hears and delivers them out of all their troubles. The Lord is near to the brokenhearted and saves the crushed in spirit." (Psalm 34:17-18).*

The bible tells us how Jesus was sent to us by God to give his life as a ransom for our sins. Does this mean that we can continue on with our sins? What about repenting, then returning to the same old ways? Today, Satan throws out a lot of distractions. He smiles when he sees the effects in our schools, churches, communities, television, and media. Because many of us are not grounded, we are baited in by Satan and don't realize it. We are judging, hating, abusing, killing, and oppressing; yet, we believe it's part of God's work. Furthermore, we still believe we are Christians. Wow! *"If anyone thinks he is religious and does not bridle his tongue but deceives his heart, this person's religion is worthless." (James 1:26).*

How do you want to live the rest of your life? As I approach the age of 50, I realize that I am far beyond the second half of my life. I want to live the remaining years in abundance, with happiness, trying to be obedient, and God-fearing. There's no need to get hung up on the past behaviors. I am bringing a new set of core values into this second half. What about you? I also realized that my mom left past disappointments, jealousy, and envious men and women behind as she approached her senior years. She also realized that people will continue to be judgmental despite their Christian beliefs. She, on the other hand, decided to pray every night and ask forgiveness for her sins. It appeared as though mom was committed to God for the last twenty-five years of her life.

Knocked Off-Balance

I hope that my mom's journey and the other stories in this book have inspired and hopefully helped you. We're all going to encounter some unexpected blows in our lives. Some will be devastating and keep you against the ropes. Fight back and don't wave the flag, quit, or throw in the towel! That's too easy. Seek help! Pray for strength and courage! Don't be tricked by Satan's deception! If nothing else, reflect on some of these stories and think to yourself, "if they can weather the storm, so can I." But, you can't do it alone.

Writing this book has become very therapeutic for me. It has also given me a spiritual uplifting. I have found it to be amazing that there's a scripture in the bible for almost any challenge that we face in life. In my eyes, that is truly God. Who else would know this? Now that you have read these compelling stories, have you realized that your situation is not as bad or worse than others. How you handle it, cope, and find resolve is what's most important. Let's not allow our lives to be determined by the unexpected blows that have knocked us off balance! Stay strong and have some courage to overcome the obstacles. If you have never prayed or asked God for guidance, give it a try. What will it hurt! He loves us all and will help us if we ask. *"I love those who love me, and those who seek me, diligently find me." (Proverbs 8:17).*

Prior to incorporating God in my life, unexpected blows

caused my knees to buckle. (Using the boxing analogy). I didn't pray for help or guidance. One more blow would drop me like a "sack of potatoes." Now that I walk with God, I'm better equipped. My **new cornerman** patches my wounds and gets me right back in the ring. *"Whether you are bracing yourself for the inevitable blow or trying to pick yourself up from one that has already been landed, Jesus is there to help you get back in the fight." One Year,* Uncommon Life, *Daily Challenge by Tony Dungy).* How about you? Are you better prepared now for the unexpected blows that may knock you off balance?

References

Bible Versions

King James Version- KJV

New King James Version -NKJV

English Standard Version-ESV

New International Version-NIV

American Standard Version-ASV

New American Standard Bible

treatment-centers.net

Wikipedia

pandys.org

Alcohol Anonymous

victimsofcrime.org

salon.com

www.ncsl.org

HelpGuide.org

fivethirtyeight.com

recoveryconnection.com

Forbes.com

www.treatmentsolutions.com

psychcentral.com

American Cancer Society

trauma.blog.yorku.ca

www.healthpovertyaction.org

Forbes and Salary.com

chicagotribune.com

U.S Drug Enforcement Administration

www.healthpovertyaction.org

Substance Abuse and Mental Health Services Administration

resurrection.wordpress.com

2008 National Survey on Drug Use and Health

Quote by Joy Behar

Quote by Maya Angelou

Webster-Merriam.com

Quote by Iyanla VanZant

psychologytoday.com

Mindfulness for Teachers by Patricia A. Jennings.

Quote by Bob Marley

Quotes from Pintrest.com

Huffington Post

Lucado, Max (2001). Traveling Light.

WebMD

Evans, Tony (2013). Kingdom Man Devotional

Cleveland, James. "I Don't Feel No Ways Tired."

Make a Wish Foundation and the Ronald McDonald House

Brown, Marvelyn (2008). Naked Truth.

Seven, starring Morgan Freeman and Brad Pitt

Community Action Project(Y-CAP) sponsored by the YMCA

The Mayo Clinic

American Psychiatric Association, January 2017

The Journal of Sexual Medicine, June 2013

MentalHealth.gov.

Medical News Today

Inc.com

LiveLiveHappy.com

Stewart Scott-ESPN

"God promotes you on your heart not your talents." Sermon by TD Jakes,

Jakes, TD (2017). <u>SOAR!</u>

Dungy, Tony June 30, July 13, Sept. 20, (2011). One Year, <u>Uncommon Life,</u> Daily Challenge.

Simon, Bryant, (2017). <u>The Hamlet Fire: A Tragic Story of Cheap Food, Cheap Government, and Cheap Lives.</u>

Quote by <u>RickThomas.net</u>

Cloke, Bill, <u>5 Ways to Rebuild Trust After It's broken</u>, Care2.

Reverend Beverly Fest, Mountain Ministry in Boulder, CO

Relationship Rules

Quote by Bernard Meltzer

Thomas, Tonya (2015). <u>Am I your enemy because I tell you the truth.</u>

MoveMe Quotes

Quote by C. Kennedy, <u>goodreads.com</u>

Payne, Ruby K. PH. D (2003)<u>. "Understanding and Working with Students and Adults from Poverty</u>".

About the Author

Clayvon Scott Sr. was born in Hamlet, NC. He is the youngest of sixteen children born to Elreta McKnight Scott, (Marie). He grew up in a poverty- stricken household. Despite poor economic conditions, his mother instilled in him the importance of God, family, treatment of others, education, and friendships. Although he would incur some embarrassment and ridicule in school as a youngster, Clayvon attracted the attention of many people with his intellect, athletic abilities, and good nature. He was a well-rounded, and well-grounded young man. Clayvon's hard work, dedication, and good nature yielded friendships with pretty girls, positive friends, and prestigious athletic awards throughout his high school years.

Clayvon earned a basketball scholarship during his senior year in high school, to attend Tennessee State University, in Nashville, Tn. There, he learned the importance of respect for people, education, and life-long friendships. The same lessons instilled by his mom throughout childhood. Tennessee State is where Clayvon met his wife. He graduated with a Bachelors in Business Administration in 1992. Clayvon got married and landed a job with his current employer, within six months after graduation. It was with these series of intentional events that he realized that, "God is an awesome God."

Clayvon's 20-year marriage produced three fine young men who are currently in college, and pursuing their dreams. He instills in them, the same morals, and values he learned from his mom. Clayvon teaches his boys that life is full of challenges that can be overcome through prayer, perseverance, and a faith filled walk with God.

Clayvon is a first-time author. He will be writing a series of inspirational and self-help books related to life's challenges. He is inspired by his mom, authors Tonya Thomas, ("Am I Your Enemy Because I Tell You the Truth"), Tony Dungy ("Uncommon Life"), and a host of family members, and friends. Clayvon's journey is lifting him up, and bringing him to a closer relationship with Jesus Christ. His series of books will encourage, and strengthen your prayer and faith in all walks throughout life.

<u>Purpose</u>

My purpose in writing this book is to help others who have encountered some of the same obstacles mentioned. They will witness how others have overcome the same types of challenges in life. Though some situations are worse than others, my book offers confirmation of the fact that, we are not alone in our journey through life. You will witness that some people are still off balance. You will also witness how others have found resolve, and ways to cope and heal. You will witness how they pressed forward, and regained balance. You will witness the inevitable truth that healing takes place over a long period of time for some and a short period for others. It requires change, prioritizing, commitment, perseverance, thought, prayer, counseling, self-motivation and most importantly, realization, an accepted truth about a life altering chain of events.

Inspiration

What inspired me to write this book was the reflection on my mom's life. It was full of unexpected events that determined her course of life. Also, witnessing my youngest son battle Depression and trying to figure out how to help him. Then, I started thinking about all the unexpected events that I've encountered in my personal life and how the changes affected me and my kid's lives. I also began to reflect on past events my family and friends went through that knocked them off balance.

Notes

Notes